REDISCOVERING RITUAL

REDISCOVERING RITUAL

Paul D. Jones, S.J.

Woodstock Center for Religion and Worship

NEWMAN PRESS

New York / Paramus / Toronto

Acknowledgment
and/or by E. E. Cummings: Copyright, 1950,
by E. E. Cummings. Reprinted from his
volume COMPLETE POEMS 1913-1962 by
permission of Harcourt Brace Jovanovich, Inc.

Library of Congress
Catalog Card Number: 73-77392

ISBN: 0-8091-0180-7

Published by Paulist Press
Editorial Office: 1865 Broadway, N.Y., N.Y. 10023
Business Office: 400 Sette Drive, Paramus, N.J. 07652

Printed and bound in the
United States of America

Contents

Introduction

About ten years ago a group of theologians met and *Time* magazine published their findings: God is dead! At approximately the same time theater people were mourning the death of that medium. Psychologists and sociologists nourished on existentialism discussed alienation and lack of communication, while educators lamented the structures that produced the vanishing adolescent. This thanatological thinking has not waned over the years and so we are presently haunted by ecological, urban and technological specters who will, if we are not extremely vigilant, mow us down with their sweeping scythes. Ours is a Bergmanesque world where light is wintry and warmth is mere fantasy.

As a protest and affirmation of this terrible human condition we should march to the World Trade Center, ride elevators to its windy heights and plummet off. But let's take a last look before we do.

Theologians are now talking about play and celebration. The theater has become participational. Psychologists are encountering and sensitizing. Sociologists are proposing alternative life styles, while educators are flourishing in mini-courses and free schools. Darkness has not triumphed; there is some light. Perhaps it is best to abandon the suicide pact for a while.

Worship, liturgy, ritual or whatever word describes the phenomenon of individual or corporate action addressed to a meaningful transcendent has also experienced prolonged death rattles. The contributing weaknesses are manifest and worthy of note.

The first weakness is hereditary and its roots can be found at some point of history in all religious families, when ritual ceased to evolve with culture and became fixed or the occupation of a few select professionals. In Catholicism, the fifteen hundred years preceding the Counter-Reformation manifested two interesting trends: a rich development of liturgical forms and a growing tendency on the part of Church authority to function as an arbiter in this growth process. Events like the forced departure of drama from the cathedral to the town square and the banning of liturgical dance by the Council of Wurzburg in 1298 foreshadowed the stagnation and professionalization of Catholic worship that followed the promulgation of the missal of Pius V (1570) and the establishment of the enforcer of its liturgical guidelines, the Sacred Congregation of Rites (1588). The renowned liturgist, Joseph Jungmann, poetically describes the full

emergence of Catholicism's hereditary disease in these words:

> After fifteen hundred years of unbroken develop-
> ment in the rite of the Roman Mass, after the rush-
> ing and the streaming from every height and out of
> every valley, the Missal of Pius V was indeed a pow-
> erful dam holding back the waters or permitting
> them to flow only in firm, well-built canals. At one
> blow all arbitrary meandering to one side or the
> other was cut off, all floods prevented, and a safe,
> regular and useful flow assured. But the price paid
> was this, that the beautiful river valley now lay bar-
> ren and the forces of further evolution were often
> channeled into the narrow bed of a very inadequate
> devotional life instead of gathering strength for new
> forms of liturgical expression. [1]

Today, after four hundred years of rubricism and even the reforms of Vatican II we are so accustomed to theologians, liturgical commissions, priests and impressarios creating our rituals that the suggestion that we should share the ritual burden is traumatic. We choose to live with the gnawing boredom of our hereditary disease and stoically profess that "worship is the responsibility of the shepherd not the sheep!"

The second weakness is much like the first as it also roots itself in a tradition which has divinized only select actions as ritualistic or worshipful. Hence, we have allowed bows, joined hands, outstretched arms, and many other familiar gestures to form the catalog of sacred actions. We question these traditional actions not nearly as often as we do our own natural ritual sense which suggests other actions as equally sacred and meaningful. In this same mind set, we have also confined ritual to special places--churches, the-aters or ball parks--and in so doing have bypassed the richness that can be found closer to home. In relation to worship, living room liturgies with their informal actions are not the panacea, they are merely a minor treatment for the disease.

The third, which is basically attitudinal, springs from and nourishes the others. Its cause is fear: a fear of emotionalism and/or ecstasy in worship, a fear of the body in ritual, a fear

---

[1] Joseph Jungmann, *The Mass of the Roman Rite: Its Origins and Devel-opment.* New York, 1950. Volume I, pp. 140-41.

that a loss of the getting-the-job-done mentality will destroy worship, a fear that enjoyment will eradicate the high supernatural motives that underpin worship, and a fear of breaking the time-proven patterns and structures of ritual. The fear which causes embarrassment at even the wishy-washy "kiss" of peace, or urges us to question the value of folk or rock liturgical music, lingers as a disease weakening individuality and creativity so that a neutral, universal, nonconfrontational worshiping being might exist. And that being is a corpse.

The fourth weakness is the most debilitating. Ritual/worship is defined as action (words, gesture, etc.) which is addressed to a transcendent (God, a power structure, etc.) that is experienced as meaningful and active in an individual's or community's life and culture. The transcendent has become, for many of us who profess to be worshiping believers, an abstract one who deserves impersonal worship structures. When a transcendent is imbedded in a man's consciousness as a vibrant, active life force, the action relating to this transcendent is truly religious or worshipful, but when a transcendent loses its immediacy it becomes myth and action becomes theater. Greek religious ritual became Greek drama and in many places Christian worship has become a type of second-rate theater. It took a great genius like Tyrone Guthrie to revitalize Greek drama and make it a compelling experience for contemporary man, and it will take an even greater genius to direct existing worship structures while their transcendent remains distant from the consciousness and experience of the people. This fourth weakness will remain as long as man continues to worship the God of Sunday obligation or the social register divinity.

Although these weaknesses are creating the death rattles in contemporary ritual, one need not, as many are suggesting, condone ritual euthanasia or take a more conservative course and pray for ritual's speedy and natural death. Rather, one must manifest the same hope and determination as artists, psychologists and educators who have conquered death by trusting in man's creative energy. Today's ritualist can heal what many consider hopeless by overcoming fear, questioning tradition, confronting professionals, revitalizing transcendents, and, most important, learning to trust and utilize the personal, communal and cultural resources that are his. As learner, the contemporary ritualist must have the freedom to bypass existing worship and sacramental structures until he has gained the knowledge and experience from the more immediate and less complex ritual structures that are a part of his life. The ritual maker, like

the director who introduced participational theater as a life force in a dying medium, must have an understanding of the foundations that support meaningful and creative rituals. The remaining considerations of this introduction and the entire book seek to uncover those foundations and stimulate the ritual creativity of the reader.

FOUNDATIONS OF RITUAL

Ritual Action

The action of ritual mirrors the transcendent to which it is addressed. In general, the ritual transcendent--a deity, force, power structure--is paradoxical. It is simultaneously present and elusive, understandable and enigmatic, personal and impersonal. The transcendent's dual nature demands ritual activity that relates to both aspects of the paradox. Hence, our experience of ritual patterns informs us that these structures employ both ordinary and symbolic language, gesture and art.

However, it is on the symbolic level that man probes the deepest, for in using symbolism he admits the failure of ordinary language, gesture and art to completely express the relationship between the transcendent and himself. It would be profitable to briefly consider the symbol to see how it exceeds ordinary expression's ability to reveal ritual man's depth.

Symbolism in Ritual

Like the transcendent, the symbol also functions on two levels. It has conventional meaning derived from nature, culture or tradition, and on this level it may be called objective. It also serves as a springboard for free association and interpretation while presenting itself as a rubric under which many different states or emotions can be gathered; on this level it may be called subjective. Reflection on our own experience reveals the objective-subjective nature of the symbol, for when we view an actor's gesture of sadness we are simultaneously aware of the objective sign and its power to elicit our own feelings of sadness. When we say God the Father we are united with all who use that title without losing the unique fatherhood that God manifests in our lives.

The problem with contemporary worship is not primarily one of ordinary expression (new translations, music or art); rather it focuses on symbolism. As we have noted, a symbol must function on two levels to have full impact. It enjoys this ability by being an active part of an individual's or community's cultural, imaginative or traditional experience.

Regal vestments represented divine or priestly dominion in a monarchical culture and were vital symbols; they are not now. Agrarian imagery, heaven-on-earth Gothic architecture, and magical gestures do not free contemporary man to probe his depths. These common worship elements are not grounded in our experience and therefore cannot function symbolically. The task of today's ritual maker is to take careful stock of the use of ordinary and symbolic expression in worship. It is not enough to merely note the conflict between contemporary idioms and a-cultural symbolism; rather, as healer and creator, he must work for a unification of the ordinary and symbolic elements of ritual. His principal guidelines in this project will be his knowledge of ritual structures, stimuli and transcendents active in his culture.

Ritual Structures in Culture

For modern man, parties, organized sports, political conventions, greetings, dating, protest marches and many other experiences are commonplace. Yet only a few individuals consciously reflect on these occurrences and note that their action is ritualistic. For example, the anti-war march which occupies much of contemporary news reporting contains a transcendent (the personal and impersonal war machine, injustice or whatever) and actions which are ordinary (marching, posters, chants) and symbolic (black arm bands, coffins, simulated napalm injury). The march allows the participant to experience group identity through conventional elements while freeing him to vent his own particular feelings of anger and frustration. The transcendent active in the protest serves to direct and focus the ritual structure. If one were to radically alter, either by design or force, one of the essential elements of the march, its dynamics and function as ritual action would be destroyed. This fundamental truth of ritual is well known to rioters and tactical police.

By way of exercise, it would be profitable to choose a familiar ritual pattern and play with its elements. Imagine the Super Bowl being played backward or drop the transcendent of nominating a candidate from a political convention. By playful experimentation with familiar ritual patterns one can easily arrive at the structural knowledge that is essential when dealing with worship.

Ritual Stimuli in Culture

Not so many years ago three bullets left three guns and killed three men. Every day bullets leave guns and kill; yet there was something special in these three killings and the entire nation mourned the passing and celebrated the greatness of these men in many ways ranging from ghetto riots to cathedral liturgies. National tragedy is not our sole ritual stimulus, for we react to all great human experiences in a way that is set apart from routine day-to-day existence. It is only when we begin to exclude certain areas of human experience as ritual stimuli that we get into the boring rut which is typical of communities that have celebrated the togetherness-brotherhood-love theme into the ground.

Because so many of us are familiar only with the limited stimuli that motivate most of our worship we are at a loss when someone or something urges us to broaden our horizons. Yet, if we were to turn to our own secular ritual experience we would not be lost. Consider, for a moment, the stimuli that motivate parties in our society. We welcome the birth of a child, we celebrate the passing of a year, we hail job promotions, we shed tears at departures and retirements, and drink and eat together after a funeral. If we add this one ritual structure to the many other familiar secular rituals, we discover that there is a gap between what we celebrate in life and in worship. The individual who knows the ritual stimuli and responses of his culture is one who can make worship a more meaningful and fulfilling experience.

The Transcendent in Ritual

We have noted in many sections of this introduction that ritual derives its energy and focus from the transcendent present in the individual or community consciousness and belief. To function effectively, the transcendent must be experienced as involved in the human process, for it is there that the stimuli for ritual action are found. The problem in most religious rituals today is that doctrine concerning the nature of the transcendent does not concur with the experience of the worshipers. The blame for this disharmony does not fall on the doctrine itself but rather on the teachers, structures and believers expressing this doctrine. Ritually speaking, the bored congregation attending a perfunctory service conducted by a distant minister is enacting "good" ritual, for the transcendent is focusing and directing activity which is ordinary and symbolic! But is this sort of "good" ritual our ideal? Hardly. To remedy this situation one needs to look at the vital transcendents that urge ritual action in

secular society. How did they receive their being? How do they grow in influence? How do they maintain their hold on so many lives? Take, for example, a recent "god" in our society, marijuana. Does it enjoy its power because some doctrine says that it is peaceloving and unifying? Newspaper stories, rock lyrics, turned-on folk heroes, rumors of legalization, testify that doctrine alone does not make a transcendent a vital part of one's consciousness. If one were to carefully study the other active transcendents of our culture, he would be more equipped to act upon Avery Dulles' words which, though directed to Catholicism, apply to all religions:

> The rich variety of modes by which Christ himself *(or any major religious leader)* communicated suggests that the Church, too, as an incarnational reality, may utilize all the possibilities of communication at hand in a given culture. [2]

STRUCTURE AND USE OF THE BOOK

The preceding considerations of ritual diseases and the foundations, which can exert both curative and creative power in ritual, were presented to provide the reader with a grounding in the dynamics and theory which prompted the creation of the six ritual events that form the major part of this book. These events, which ritualize basic life situations, have been successfully performed and, in several instances, modified by various secular and religious communities. Each ritual can be used in its entirety as a text for a particular event, or a section of any ritual might be used in itself or as an addition to an existing ritual structure. Primarily, these six rituals that follow should be used as guidelines for the individual and/or communal creation of new events. To assist in this goal, each event is prefaced by a brief note concerning its cultural ground, transcendent and structure, and each is also followed by a list of suggestions as to how the event might be modified or be used experimentally. To further the primary goal of the book, a final rather detailed and analytic chapter has been included as a program guide for the creation and evaluation of new rituals. Since this concluding chapter relies heavily on the experience and knowledge gained in the performance of the six ritual events, it cannot

[2]Avery Dulles, "The Church as Multimedia," *New Catholic World*, Vol. 215, No. 1282, Jan-Feb., 1972, p. 22.

be used apart from the events as a short-cut to creative ritual making.

Abbie Hoffman titled his work *Steal This Book* and in so doing aptly described his counter-cultural philosophy. With the same philosophical pithiness in mind this volume might be subtitled: *Perform This Book*.

Chapter One
Initiation-Birth/Re-Birth Event

CULTURAL GROUND

Throughout history, man has always formally-ritually welcomed his fellow man into a specific sect, way of life or new responsibility. As Christians, we are not set apart from other religious or cultural practices, for while we are baptizing and confirming, Jews are conferring bar mitzvah, Bantus are performing adolescent circumcisions and secular society is initiating its members into clubs, political parties, fraternities--into any state that demands a particular behavioral response.

What has always happened and continues to happen in initiation rituals is that a certain group of individuals, the initiated or proficients, screen, test and train the un-initiates until they are judged worthy to accept the responsibility that comes with membership in the sect or club.

Even though the screening, testing and responsibilities of each initiation vary in depth, there is a unifying pattern evident in each. The familiar event of Christian baptism serves us as a model for all initiation rites. Baptism, which is the formalized/ritualized welcoming of an individual into an initiated community, moves through these stages:

Screening: The individual himself, or, in the case of infants, his sponsors, are questioned concerning Christian life and responsibility. It is helpful to note that the present screening process is a mere sketch of the powerful screening of adult (infant baptism was not practiced) candidates--catechumens--in the early Church! When the candidate is approved, the formal initiation process containing three movements begins.

The First Movement relates the candidate to his past: you were once under the dominion of Satan, a creature of darkness and so forth.

The Second Movement brings the candidate into the present: by the pouring of the baptismal water you are out of Satan's grasp and are a Son of God.

The Third Movement, relating to the future, was more present in the early Church practices of conferring baptism, confirmation and Eucharist together at the Easter Vigil. The future element is only seminally present in current baptismal practices (via promises and exhortations) because it is a focal point of confirmation when the initiate accepts the responsibility of Christian mission.

In his book, *Feast of Fools,* Harvey Cox describes celebration in terms of festivity, fantasy and man's taking time out from making history. The initiation rite manifests these elements:

it is festive in that it relates man to his past history--where he has been;

it is fantastic in that it heightens his awareness of himself as a being who has come from history to this moment of time when he can hope and dream about the future--where he will go;

it is time out because in a moment that is set apart from day-to-day existence he experiences a rare phenomenon of time converging to reveal the totality of his being.

Cox reserves celebration to religious man, who believes in a being or force who possesses sufficient power to ground man in his project from past through present to future. It is in celebration-ritual that man joins with other men to meet this power. [1]

[1] Harvey Cox, *Feast of Fools.* Cambridge, 1969. It would be profitable for the reader to flesh out the skeletal form of Cox's argument by carefully reading the entire volume.

As we move through subsequent events, we trust that the reader will note their explicit or implied celebratory framework.

THE TRANSCENDENT

Although we are positing a Christian God in this event, any force or ideal which manifests the unifying goal of the community will suffice. However, it must be stated that the more comprehensive the transcendent the more sophisticated and deep the ritual. Hence, we experience baptism and confirmation on a different level than membership in the country club, because the transcendent in the religious events affects the totality of man's existence while membership touches only the social aspect of his life.

STRUCTURE

The initiation event derives its structure from the dynamics presented above. Following a period of preparation or screening which can be a part of the ritual itself, the candidates are led through three movements (past-present-future) that are unified by the transcendent grounding the initiation process. The structure of every initiation event and of every ritual must be flexible enough to allow each participant his own response to the ritual action, yet it must provide sufficient control to focus each participant on the goal of the ritual process. The freedom-control tension of ritual will be discussed at length in the final chapter so that the reader who has performed the six events may be more disposed to grapple with the problem it presents.

CHRISTIAN MATURITY EVENT

The following Christian maturity event concretizes the general principles of the initiation event presented above. It posits a transcendent who calls each individual from a state of childish playfulness to be initiated into responsible Christian witness. The event is similar to the sacrament of confirmation or ordination but its scope also includes the processes of rededication and reconversion. Structurally, the event is standard and like many initiation rites it chooses to incorporate the screening process into the past-present-future orientation of the event.

PARTICIPANTS:
Candidates: Adolescents, young adults, recent con-

verts, or anyone seeking to rededicate himself to the principles of the Gospel.

Ministers: Mature Christians of every vocation whose lives evidence a commitment to Christ and his Gospel. This group consists of a leader, chosen by lot or office, and a sponsor for each candidate.

THE PLACE: A large space which can be divided into two completely separate areas. Two spacious rooms will do, as will the vestibule and sanctuary/chancel of a church.

MATERIALS:

Crosses or other Christian symbols for all participants in the event.

Bibles (Old and New Testaments): one for the leader and one gift wrapped for each candidate.

Toys, games, noisemakers, party hats, catechetical literature for the vestibule area--a more detailed list can be found in the text of Part I (Past).

Candles and posters depicting Christian commitment for the sanctuary area--more suggestions given in the text.

ACTION OF THE EVENT

The Past

Candidates and ministers gather in the brightly lighted vestibule area where they are surrounded by objects representing the life they are about to leave. The objects, ranging from catechetical literature and posters to party-fun objects: bubble soap, party hats, games, Hawaiian leis (literature and fun objects will be determined by the age of the candidates), should be used to create a carefree atmosphere in the vestibule area. If it is possible, several working televisions and a loud stereo should be used to add to the excitement that should be present in the room. If the candidates do not spontaneously get into the party spirit, the ministers should initiate games and try to involve the candidates in the experience of carefree existence or being entertained that is the preparatory dynamic for the event. When the party atmosphere has taken hold, ministers should begin to depart from the vestibule area in intervals--one by one so that their leaving does not break the mood. After each minister leaves the vestibule space he goes immediately into the sanctuary space where he prays silently for the candidates.

The sanctuary space should stand in contrast to the vestibule. It should be dimly lighted and contain a simple table with an open Bible and a few lighted candles on it and post-

ers or banners depicting the Christian life. While distraction is the purpose of the decorations and objects of the vestibule space, simplicity and understatement is the ideal here.

When all of the ministers have gathered in the sanctuary space, the leader calls them forward and instructs them to form a circle around the table containing the candles and Bible. When the ministers are positioned the leader picks up the Bible, opens it and begins:

Leader:

And all who believed were gathered together and had all things in common. They sold their possessions and goods and shared them with the needy. And every day, attending the temple together and breaking bread in their homes, they partook of food with glad and generous hearts, praising God and having favor with all the people. And the Lord added to their number, day by day, those who were being saved.

(Acts 2:44-47)

When the reading is over the leader replaces the Bible on the table and chooses one of the ministers, saying: The peace of the Lord is with you.

The chosen minister responds: "His peace is also with you," and goes to the vestibule area where he finds the candidate he is sponsoring. He brings him into the sanctuary area and instructs him to stand behind the table containing the Bible. He stands next to his candidate.

Note:

This process of the minister-sponsor being chosen and presenting his candidate(s) is repeated after the first candidate is initiated. The Acts reading is omitted as a preparation to subsequent initiations.

The Present

The sponsor (minister) turns to his candidate and addresses him.

Minister:

We would like to welcome you into a community of Christians who are trying to live their lives as loving and responsible followers of Jesus Christ. Are you willing to partake in the welcoming ceremony we have prepared for you?

Candidate:

Responds ad lib to the question.

If the candidate refuses to undergo the process, he is thanked and blessed by each of the ministers. He then may return to the group in the vestibule or leave.

If he assents, the process continues.

Leader (moving to a position facing the candidate):
Tell us how you would try to live out your life as a mature Christian man/woman.
Candidate:
Responds freely; following his answer, a series of questions or instructions should come from the ministers listening to him. If for example the candidate states that he will live out his life in the service of his fellow man, a process like the following might begin:
Minister 1:
Do you understand that the service you describe involves sacrifice?
Candidate:
Yes I do.
Minister 3 (or 4, 5, . . .):
Do you believe that there is anything in addition to serving your fellow man that would mark you as a committed Christian?
Candidate:
Yes, I think that the Christian has an obligation to make sure that his Church addresses the needs of the world in a manner that is more than verbal.
Minister 6:
Could you explain this?
The questioning process should not attempt to tyrannize the individual; rather it should help clarify his beliefs. It should be allowed to continue until the candidate and ministers have established rapport. When the leader judges that the process has fulfilled its purpose, he addresses the candidate:
Leader:
N., you have answered the questions well. Please listen carefully to the words your sponsor will read to you:
Minister:
Men have different gifts, but it is the same Spirit who gives them. There are different ways of serving God, but it is the same Lord who is served. God works through different men in different ways, but it is the same God who achieves his purpose through them all. Each man is given his gift by the Spirit that he may use it for the common good.

(1 Cor. 12:4-8)

Leader:
(to Candidate) Your presence here today (tonight) testifies to your gift and your words affirm your desire to use it for the common good. Yet, if you were to read further in this letter from St. Paul, you

would discover that the Christian does not flaunt his gift independently, but rather supports and encourages all to share their gifts with a common goal in mind. Paul calls the unifying gift of all Christians charity or love. For the Christian it is not enough to merely love God; he must love his brother.

Love as we experience it manifests itself in need of and trust in one's fellow man. Scripture tells us: He who says that he loves God, while hating his fellow man, is a liar.

Are you willing to symbolize your trust in and need for the support of your fellow Christians?
Candidate:
Responds ad lib yes/no (if negative, he departs, as above; if affirmative, the event continues).

Sponsor blindfolds his candidate and leads him into the center of the circle of ministers. At this point, one of many trust activities should take place. For example: the candidate could be led on a "blind" walk by each minister who would give him instructions in the process so that he would not be injured, or the candidate could stand rigidly in the center of a tight circle of ministers and fall backward, letting the ministers break his fall. This exercise can be repeated several times.

Note:
The nature of the exercise depends on the age of the candidate.

When the exercise is over, the candidate is returned to the center of the circle and his blindfold is removed. Leader addresses him:

Leader:
(The following is an example of what should be improvised.)
N., the action which you just performed may have been difficult for you. If so, remember that it was only symbolic, and that as a mature Christian you will be asked to act with trust and love in real situations that might be far more difficult and taxing. If the action was enjoyable, it is only a glimmer of the deep joy that parallels the hardship of the Christian life.

(The following could be improvised, but it is essential that the points of mature Christian responsibility and acceptance be maintained.)

Because by your words and actions you have manifested a readiness to accept the responsibilties of mature Christianity, we are happy to say that we

need, trust and welcome you as a brother/sister in Christ Jesus our Lord.

Sponsor removes party hat and Hawaiian lei from candidate (if he is wearing them) and silently lays hands on the candidate's head. When he has done this he picks up the Bible and reads. (The remaining ministers silently lay on hands during the reading.)

Sponsor:

Delight yourself in the Lord; yes, find your joy in him at all times. Have a reputation for kindness. Don't worry over anything: tell God every detail of your needs in sincere and thankful prayer. And the peace of God, which exceeds all human understanding, will keep constant guard over your heart and mind as it rests in Christ Jesus.

(Phil. 4:4-8)

When the reading and laying on of hands is over, the candidate is given a gift-wrapped Bible and a symbol of his new position. It would be most appropriate if each of the ministers were to wear a cross and that the new minister be given a similar cross.

The Future

The leader blesses the new minister.

Leader:

Bring peace to the world, have courage and hold on to what is good. Support the weak, help the suffering, love the unloved. Serve the Lord always and rejoice in the power of the Holy Spirit.

And the Lord will bless and keep you.

He will be kind to you and grant you peace.

May almighty God bless you: the Father and the Son and the Holy Spirit.

Minister:

Amen.

Leader:

As a sign of your new ministry you will join with us in the initiation of the remaining candidates.

(Obviously the wording would be altered should this be the only or last initiation rite.)

The new minister is informally welcomed at this point and, depending on whether there are more candidates, the event either continues or concludes. If the event continues, the same past-present-future movement repeats itself; if it concludes, the following takes place:

Conclusion

Leader begins improvised petitional prayers (the following are guidelines):

Leader:

Let us pray (moment of silence).

For the brothers and sisters who have been welcomed here today, that they may continue to grow in the service of Christ and his Church,

All:

We pray to the Lord. (Hear us, O Lord; or another response)

Leader:

For all people who are striving to live their life in Christ Jesus,

All:

We pray. . .

(At this point, the leader may invite others to pray, and when petitions come to an end the leader continues with a concluding prayer which should be improvised: the following are suggestions.)

Leader:

God our Father, we thank you for Christ our Lord and Brother and the Spirit who gifts us all. But especially, we are most thankful for the great love you have manifested in these men and women, who have pledged themselves to your service. For these special gifts and all the wonders of our lives, we praise and thank you today and every day. Amen.

and/or

i thank You God for most this amazing
day:for the leaping greenly spirits of trees
and a blue true dream of sky;and for everything
which is natural which is infinite which is yes

(i who have died am alive again today,
and this is the sun's birthday;this is the birth
day of life and of love and wings:and of the gay
great happening illimitably earth)

how should tasting touching hearing seeing
breathing any-lifted from the no
of all nothing-human merely being
doubt unimaginable You?

(now the ears of my ears awake and
now the eyes of my eyes are opened)

e.e. cummings

(The first stanza alone serves nicely as a simple prayer of praise.)

Following the concluding prayer of the event, it is most appropriate to have a party or a dinner welcoming the new ministers.

SUGGESTIONS FOR ADAPTATION

1.

The event may be performed for a community which, after having passed through the vestibule area, could be seated either in the sanctuary area or in another space (e.g., in the pews).

2.

In an actual event, a minister might have more than one candidate. If this is the case, the group should go through each phase of the ritual together rather than one at a time with the others as spectators. Questions or actions in each phase of the event should be directed to each member of the group.

3.

A Eucharist could easily be substituted for the concluding dinner or party. It should begin with an offertory where each new minister verbally offers his specific talent/gift to the assembled community. The verbal offering might be underscored by the new minister's placing of his cross upon the altar: the remaining ministers could join in this activity.

4.

If the number of candidates is quite large, several sanctuary areas, groups of ministers, and attending communities could be used for the initiation of candidates. One large vestibule space would suffice, as the more crowded and alive this area is, the more it contributes to the dynamic of the event. All groups should gather in one area for the concluding petitional prayers.

5.

If the event is to be used as a reconversion/rededication ritual, the initial questioning of Part I should be changed to include the notion of turning away from sin and selfishness to a new life in Christ. The questioning/instruction should not focus on the sin of the candidate, for his presence in the rite suggests penitence; rather the questioning ministers should help him determine or express the new course his life will take.

6.

Symbolization or physicalization of the verbal element is a powerful force in ritual action. If, for example, the candidate

in this event describes his Christian life (Part I) as service, it is effective to ask him to perform an on-the-spot symbolic act (e.g., washing the ministers' feet, reading a text, etc.) or promise to do some sort of volunteer work after the event.

Chapter Two
Consolidation Event

CULTURAL GROUND

In most civilizations, various times of the year were chosen to recharge and focus the individual and group energy of the people. These times and their events were natural follow-ups to the initiation rites, for the ritualists knew that enthusiasm and commitment vanished without continuing support. These events were generally an annual occurrence, and, like Lent, they took place in the spring when nature and man could experience the process of growth together. If we only have a TV movie anthropologist's knowledge, we know that the American Indian danced before hunting the buffalo or making war on the invading white man as a means of building up that energy that produced food and scalps. If we play team sports, we "psych up" before the game . . . and who doesn't have a skull session with his partner before a big bridge game? Whether our experience be grounded in religion, movies or games, we should be aware that consolidation events are as much a part of our culture as initiations.

THE TRANSCENDENT

We know from an experience like Lent that a good consolidation event must stimulate the individual's energy and channel it toward the building up of the community and its ideal. Hence, in Lent we are reminded of the boundless love of God for us manifested in Christ's redemptive activity (the transcendent) and we are also reminded of our individual and communal failure to live up to the ideal presented by Christ. We are asked to spend the period beginning in the cold of late winter, and culminating in the new life of spring, in prayer and activity that turns us away from sin/death and returns us to selflessness/life in Christ. The consolidation ritual of Lent directs man in a ritualistic re-presentation of the individual and communal redemptive activity of Christ. The ritual makes redemption a now phenomenon, and its annual occurrence reminds us that it is an on-going process. In every instance it is celebration, for man in the present as justified recalls that he was once not so gifted, and that simultaneous present-past consciousness gives him hope in the future.

Lent, like ancient Greek agrarian festivals and the Hebrew Passover celebration, is a classic consolidation ritual deriving its power and energy from a transcendent who really touches the lives of the believers.

STRUCTURE

Consolidation rituals are generally divided into two phases: a stimulating of individual energies and a focusing of those energies on some communal ideal or project/mission. If either phase of the structure is neglected the total ritual suffers. The Kent State riots are an example of excellent stimulation/motivation with no focus. The propagandist ballet of Red China testifies to the boredom resulting when the ideal is too focused. The structure of the consolidation event must avoid both extremes!

ENVIRONMENT EVENT

Today, much is being made of man's responsibility for his environment. The Christian shares in this human venture, but he is further mandated by Scripture to be a creator and to prepare all creation for the coming of the Lord (cf. Rom. 8:18ff.).

This event seeks to dramatize the creative obligations of the individual Christian and the believing community. It is designed to stimulate and focus Christian ecological consciousness.

PARTICIPANTS:
Leader: a priest or member of the community wearing an alb.
Two Readers: male and female.
Representatives: ten or more individuals chosen from the community and instructed on their roles before the event. They may be dressed uniformly, e.g., all black, to set them apart from other participants.
Musicians: singers to lead community music. Guitar, piano or organ accompaniment may be used.
Community: any number of individuals.

THE PLACE: (like the initiation event)
"Vestibule" area cleared of chairs containing a central large uncovered table.
"Sanctuary" area cleared of chairs, benches, etc., containing a central large cloth-covered table.

SEATING: either in a circle around the sanctuary table--in which case the sanctuary would have to be large enough to contain chairs for the community while keeping a lot of space open around the table. OR in the front pews of the church.
Note: The event need not take place in a church if more flexible space is available elsewhere.

MATERIALS:
For leader: Bible and text of the event.
For readers: Book of Daniel.
For representatives: Before event: texts of the event, with brief passages they are to memorize, i.e., Psalm 8.
For the event: bowls of dirty water, car fenders, broken furniture, several large cardboard boxes, trash--*more detailed listing provided in text.*
For community: only if absolutely necessary: sheets with words to songs.
In vestibule: on large table, a large bowl of fresh water, grain, flowers, natural foods, beeswax candles--*more given in text.*
In sanctuary: nothing more than a large covered table.

IN VESTIBULE SPACE

(Before the event, the following objects are placed on the vestibule table: a large bowl of fresh water, green plants and branches, a bowl of earth, rocks, natural grain, flowers, honey, several beeswax candles [to be lit immediately before the event begins]. One may add other natural objects--e.g., a small potted tree or vegetables to this list.)

The leader and two readers greet the people as they enter; they instruct them to remain in the vestibule area. Representatives are not present in this part of the event. When the people are assembled, the leader, flanked by the readers, moves behind the table and addresses the people. (He might have to take a moment to arrange the community so that they can clearly see what will take place.)

Leader: The peace and blessings of the Lord be always with you.

Community:

And also with you.

Leader:

(guideline for opening address)

We have gathered to celebrate the great gift of dominion over creation that God our Father has given us.

I welcome you to this celebration and ask that you now welcome your neighbor who shares this great gift with you.

(Pause for people to greet one another)

Before you, on the table, are many things which God has given you. Like yourselves they will someday be united with the Father, the source of creation. And like yourselves, these things need direction if they are to glorify God.

You, as the followers of Christ and the inspired of the Holy Spirit, have been given the mission of directing and returning these things (points to table) and the whole of creation to God your Father.

Please take a moment to silently reflect on this mission.

Leader:

(continues after silence)

God, our Father,
we, your sons and daughters,
accept the wonderful power and mission
you have given to us.

We will bring these gifts to your altar, trusting that you will continue to bless and help us and all of your creation.

The leader picks up an object and hands it to one of the readers; he hands another object to the other reader. He then begins to hand objects to the members of the community. When several objects have been handed out, the readers begin a procession to the sanctuary space. The community follows their lead; the leader is the last person in the procession.

IN SANCTUARY SPACE

When the readers reach the sanctuary area they pass through an opening in the circle of chairs (we presume this seating here) and place their objects on the table; the people follow their lead. The readers sit in two chairs in the circle behind the table and leave a chair between them for the leader. The people sit ad lib in the circle. The leader is the last person to place his gift and be seated.

The singers should start music (e.g., Spiritual: "He's Got the Whole World"; Psalm 122:"How I Rejoiced," Paul Quinlan's version; Folk Song: "This Land Is Your Land") at the beginning of the procession and continue it for a while after the leader has been seated. The community should join in the singing.

When the entrance song is over, the leader rises and approaches the gift-covered table:

Leader:
(Holding up large bowl of clear water)
Let us pray.
(moment of silence)
God our Father,
you have given us all of creation
as a sign of your presence.
In this clear, clean water
we are blessed and marked
with your life-giving power.

(He replaces the bowl, picks up a green branch, dips it in the clear water, turns to the readers and sprinkles them with the water.)
The readers stand and move to either side of the altar.
Reader I:
(to the people)
Please respond "Bless the Lord" to each of the following acclamations:

Note:
During the acclamations and responses, the leader will continue his blessing. He should sprinkle small groups of people with the water as well as several of the objects on the table. He stands behind the table when he has completed the blessing.

Acclamations (Book of Daniel 3:57-87 is the source) are in the form of a litany; they should be done rhythmically with the readers' acclamations tagged on to the ending of the people's responses.

Reader I and II: (in unison) All of creation,

Community: Bless the Lord.

Reader I: Angels and saints,

Community: Bless . . .

Reader II: Heaven and earth,

Community: Bless . . .

Reader I: Sun and moon,

Community: Bless . . .

Reader II: Nights and days,

Community: Bless . . .

Reader I: Mountains and hills,

Community: Bless . . .

Reader II: Seas and rivers,

Community: Bless . . .

Reader I: Plants and animals,

Community: Bless . . .

Reader II: Cities and towns,

Community: Bless . . .

Reader I: All you men,

Community: Bless . . .

Reader II: All you women,

Community: Bless . . .

Readers I and II: O let all things

Community: Bless the Lord.

Note:
The litany should be expanded; the above is merely a sample demonstrating the technique involved.

When the litany is over the leader immediately proclaims
Psalm 8:
> *Leader:*
> O Lord our God,
> how glorious is your name over all the earth!
>
> Children praise your majesty
> and their song silences your enemies.
>
> When I look at the heavens
> --the moon and the stars you have made--
> I am amazed.
> Compared to these, what is man
> that you should love him so.
>
> You have made man a little less
> than the angels.
>
> You have given him glory and honor.
>
> He rules over all of your creation:
> the beasts of the field,
> the birds of the air
> and the fishes of the sea.
>
> O Lord our God,
> how glorious is your name over all the earth!

At the conclusion of the psalm, the group of representatives
enters in procession carrying objects which show man's de-
structive powers: car fenders, discarded bottles, cans, furniture, jars of polluted water, and several large cardboard
boxes. They come into the sanctuary, face the seated community and address them:
> *Representatives:* (they should speak simultaneously
> but not in unison; they should repeat the phrase.)
> What is man that you should love him so?

Following this question, the representatives place the de-
structive objects with the gifts on the sanctuary table. They
should dump the dirty water into the clean water, extin-
guish candles, place discarded bottles with the food—in
brief, they should mar the beauty of the gifts.

When the destruction is over, the representatives gather
behind the altar and in unison, and quite sadly and quietly,
recite Psalm 8.
(Recitation followed by silence)

The representatives surround the table and sit down. The
leader rises from his seat and addresses the community:
> *Leader:*
> God our Father,

we have abused the earth and all of your creation.
Where beauty once proclaimed your presence,
ugliness remains.

We are destroying air, water and all living things
in the name of progress.
We, who have sinned against nature,
confess our failures

Please respond: "Help us create and renew, O Lord"
to each of the petitions.

Leader:
We are the dying rivers, the dying air, the vanishing
forests and animals.

Community:
Help us create and renew, O Lord!

Leader:
We are the waste, the garbage, the cans and bottles
along the highways.

Community:
Help us . . .

Leader:
We are the ghettos and their cockroaches and rats.

Community:
Help us . . .

Leader:
We are the electric can openers, the belching factor-
ies, the brown-outs and black-outs.

Community:
Help us . . .

Leader:
We are the surplus grain in Kansas and rising food
prices.

Community:
Help us . . .

Leader:
We are the poisoned swordfish and tuna, the oil-
stained beaches, the soot on windowsills.

Community:
Help us . . .

Leader:
(holding up some of the objects on the table)
We are all these things, O Lord.

Community:
Help us . . .

At the conclusion of the petitions, the leader addresses the people in words like the following:
Leader:
The destruction before you on this table could easily be overlooked. We could merely sing a song and retire to our homes, leaving the mess here for others to clean up. Or we could fill these boxes (cardboard ones brought in by the representatives) with what is destroyed, and attempt to return the table to the state it once enjoyed. I ask you to join with me, the readers and these people (pointing to the representatives), in transforming the ugliness before us.
The leader, readers, and representatives begin the process. Flowers could be placed in the discarded bottles, candles could be relit--in general, people should use their imaginations in this process. When the work is complete, the leader calls for a moment of silence and instructs people to remain where they are.
Leader:
Please listen to these words from St. Paul:

The sufferings of the present times are nothing compared with the glory to be revealed
in every one of us.

Indeed the whole of creation eagerly awaits
the revelation of the sons of God.

Like us, creation was once subject to futility,
but it now has hope because it will be freed
from its slavery to corruption
and share in the glorious freedom
of the children of God . . . .

We know that God makes all things work together,
for the good he has decreed is theirs.
(Rom. 8:18-25, adapted)

Leader:
(addressing the people directly)
You are the children of the new creation. You are strengthened by the Holy Spirit as you join with Christ in returning the whole of creation to the Father.

Take an object from the table and bring it into your home. Let it serve as a reminder of your responsibility as creators.

For you and all the wonderful things of this world
are made holy and blessed in the name of the Father
and of the Son and of the Holy Spirit.

Community:
Amen.

The leader, as in the beginning of the event, begins to hand
out objects. The readers begin a procession out of the church
and the people and the leader follow carrying their gifts.

The singers should lead the people in a procession song:
e.g., "Brand New Day" (Paul Quinlan); popular song:
"There's a New World Coming"; hymn: "Praise God From
Whom All Blessings Flow"
(Old One Hundredth).

SUGGESTIONS FOR ADAPTATION

1.
The event could be done outdoors, and the cleaning up
could be extended to include things in the area of the neighborhood. (Cf. suggestion 3 for an abbreviated version.)
2.
Part One of the event, ending in the representatives' recitation of Psalm 8, could be used in itself as a means of stimulating the ecological consciousness of the community.
3.
Part Two of the event could be used as a separate action for
a neighborhood clean-up. The leader and participants could
meet in a deserted junk-filled city lot, and, following a moment of silence, the leader could start the petitional prayers.
The clean-up would follow and Romans 8:18ff. could be used
as the conclusion of the event.
4.
A brief slide show depicting world destruction, e.g., bombed-
out villages, polluted rivers, dying wildlife, smoggy cities,
etc., presented simultaneously with the representatives' de-
structive act, would work well. A parallel slide presentation,
showing man's transformation of the environment, would fit
in nicely with the people's cleaning up of the table and sanctuary.

Chapter Three
Commitment/Vocation Event

CULTURAL GROUND

At some time in our cinema or reading experience we have
come across tales from the Arthurian legends where knights
like Gawain or Lancelot prove their strength and then go out
to find the Holy Grail or rescue the captive princess. Preceding this mission were a series of ascetic practices and jousts
that gave the knight the necessary credentials to proclaim
his vocation as champion and have that choice affirmed by
the king and his court. In legend, we find many ceremonies
held to celebrate the great champion and to send him off on
his glorious quest.

We find many such vocation rituals occurring in less fan-
ciful situations, for we know about the call and mission of
Moses, Christ, St. Paul and Jean d'Arc. In more modern
times we have testimony of call, careful preparation, commitment and mission in the lives of great men like Martin
Luther King and Malcolm X.

One need only attend a departure ceremony for VISTA or
Peace Corps volunteers or sit in the audience at a law or
medical school graduation to find expressed our culture's ritual need to hail the champions.

THE TRANSCENDENT

In most vocation rituals the transcendent is expressed as a
religious, societal or humanitarian goal: "Go therefore and
teach all nations, baptizing . . . ." "Defeat the dragon/en-
emy," or "Feed the hungry and heal the sick." Whatever the
goal, every vocation ritual seeks to provide greater solidarity

32

for the community or culture. The medieval or Roman warrior defeated a foe who threatened existence and the contemporary married couple create the family in support of society's most basic unit. In any vocation ritual, the goal/ideal-transcendent must be kept clearly present as a motivational force (the great religious leaders retiring for solitary prayer), for when it fades from consciousness the champion languishes (Aeneas and Dido).

Perhaps more than any other period in history, ours is a vocation-centered culture, for phrases like career opportunities, job corps, and in-service training are common. Although the goals of any vocation can serve as a ritual transcendent, it must be remembered that the more lives the transcendent touches, the more culturally comprehensive, unifying, and engaging the ritual. Compare troop departures in World War II with current Vietnam send-offs!

STRUCTURE

Reflection on the present and historical vocation rituals reveals this structure: a period of routing existence of open-ended possibility is interrupted by a problem-goal-ideal which causes a person (or group) to reflect on his life style. Reflection, which involves self-discipline, self-evaluation, and often prayer, leads to the moment of choice when the person affirms his power to attain the goal or to commit himself to the proposed ideal. The person then presents himself to an individual or community as worthy or prepared to undertake the mission. He is either rejected, accepted or instructed to prepare more and re-present himself. If he is accepted, he is sent forth to accomplish what he says he can do; this acceptance and sending is a great cause for celebration.

In this structure the same past-present-future dynamic (problem/preparation-presentation-mission) noted in the initiation rite is active. As was true in the initiation event, the present is the focal point here, for in it time and the energies of the chosen individual and his community meet. The witnesses to the vocation event must feel that they are a real part of the champion's life and that his concerns are theirs. His past is their own; his choice and commitment revitalizes theirs; their hopes for the future are placed with his.

CONTEMPORARY VOCATION/ COMMITMENT EVENT

Our secular experience of vocation rituals is rich, especially in the political arena where "champions" who have been called and have prepared themselves present their strategy for defeating the dragon (poverty, war, high taxes . . .) and are either accepted or rejected by the society they want to represent. Politics is a very engaging vocation ritual. Unfortunately the same cannot be said of most of our religious commitment events. People choosing a way of life do not, after their preparation, present their credentials to the community at large, nor is there more than the remotest possibility that they will have to prove their worth before receiving communal acceptance. Because so much of this proving is done in rectory offices or behind seminary walls, the vital and engaging ritual tension of acceptance-rejection is absent in religious events. While keeping within the structural guidelines for any vocation event, the following Christian marriage celebration seeks to at least symbolically introduce the ritual tension mentioned above. It strives to emphasize Christian marriage as an important vocation in the Christian community rather than treat it as a nice conventional ceremony that takes place on a warm June day.

(Note: Since this event utilizes all the participants and trappings of traditional weddings, a listing of materials is not necessary.)

PRIOR TO THE EVENT

Included in the wedding invitation will be a brief written statement by both the bride and groom as to why they seek to enter into Christian marriage. In addition to this statement, a brief biographical paragraph should be included for those who might not know one of the parties. The statements and biographies serve to personally identify those invited with the couple and to begin an energy that will become a dynamic in the marriage event.

THE EVENT

After the congregation has been seated the ushers retire to a room where the female attendants have gathered. The bride and groom, dressed in normal attire (dress and suit) enter with the priest who is dressed in a suit or simple alb. They move to the entrance of the sanctuary and face the congregation. The priest stands in the center with the bride on his

right and the groom on his left. There should be no music accompanying this entrance and positioning.

Priest:
(to congregation)
Welcome.

You have all received invitations and written statements from N. and N. They now stand before you, to seek your approval of their vocation as man and wife in the Christian community. On your behalf I will now ask each of them a few questions concerning the life they seek to enter.

(To bride):
Why do you love N.?

(To groom):
Why do you love N.?

(To bride):
You realize that as a married person you are joined with others who have chosen that life. What do you expect of them?

(To groom):
What can you and N. offer to other married couples?

(To bride or groom):
If your marriage is blessed with children how will you and N. relate to them?

(To bride):
What is the place of Christ in your marriage?

(To groom):
Why have you sought marriage in the Church?

Note:
The list of questions can be expanded and members of the congregation might also be invited to ask questions. The bride and groom should not be given a list of questions before the ceremony; rather they should be given guidelines as to the sort of question that might be asked.

Priest:
(to community)
You have heard N. and N.'s responses to the questions I have asked them. I ask that you silently pray over and ponder their responses and the words that they have written.

(*Long* period of silence)

Will all of you who approve of the Christian vocation

of N. and N. please stand and applaud as a sign of
your approval.

(Priest will allow applause to die out naturally.
Then he continues.)

Priest:
Let us pray.
(Silence)
God our Father,
N. and N. stand before you
approved by your Church and your people.
Please bless them in every way.
Let the love and beauty that they have shown us
today
shine as a bright light for the eyes of all men to see.
This we ask through Christ our Brother and Lord
who gifts us with the Holy Spirit
now and for all times to come.

(Prayer may be improvised)

All:
Amen.

Priest:
(to couple's parents)
Would the parents (and relatives) of the bride and
groom please bring them their wedding attire.

They bring up gown, tuxedo, flowers, etc., embrace or kiss
the couple and return to their seats. The maid of honor and
best man could be present to take the attire to the dressing
area.

Priest:
N. and N., receive this blessing and prepare your-
selves for the wedding celebration.
May the Father bless you with peace.
May the Son increase your love.
May the Holy Spirit gift you with a long and happy
life.

Couple:
Amen.
They retire to the dressing areas where they will put on the
wedding attire. The bride's attendants will assist. The best
man will assist the groom.

Priest:
(to congregation)

N. and N. have selected readings and songs that express their love for one another and their thoughts about the vocation they have chosen to enter today. Pray for them as you listen to the selections they have chosen.

The secular readings and songs take place here rather than in the Liturgy of the Word where too much reading tends to break a mood.

Sample Readings:
"On Friendship," from *The Prophet,* Kahlil Gibran.
Taming sequence from *The Little Prince,* Antoine de St. Exupery.
Sonnet #43 by Elizabeth Barrett Browning.

Sample Songs:
Here, There and Everywhere: The Beatles.
The Impossible Dream: Man of La Mancha.
You've Got a Friend: Carole King.

Note:
The number of readings and songs can be determined beforehand to give the couple time to dress. Members of the congregation should have been chosen to do the readings.

During the final song, the priest puts on vestments which have been placed on a bench in the sanctuary. The altar/sanctuary is decorated for the ceremony: i.e., flowers, banners, lighted candles.

When the song is over, the priest comes to the center of the sanctuary (in front of the altar) and instructs the congregation to rise.

The entrance hymn begins and the wedding party processes down the main aisle of the church. The party should form a semi-circle in the sanctuary in front of the chairs facing the congregation. Three chairs (for the couple and the priest) should be placed in front of the altar.

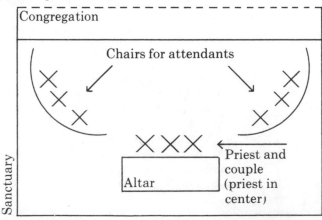

The couple should meet the priest in the center of the sanctuary and move with him to the chairs. When all are in place, all should sit except the priest who will conduct the Liturgy of the Word:

> *Priest:*
> (in place facing community)
> Let us pray.
> (period of silence)
> God our Father,
> we ask that the words from Scripture
> that we are about to hear
> may serve to strengthen N. and N.
> and all of us who are trying to serve you.
> This we ask through Christ and the Holy Spirit . . . .
>
> (Prayer may be improvised)
>
> *All:*
> Amen.

The readings should be brief: e.g., Epistle: 1 John 4:7-13 (developing the theme of love of God and love of man as marks of the Christian) and read by a member of the congregation; Gospel (read by the priest): Mt. 4:14-7 (developing the theme of Christian witness) The priest should follow the readings with a brief homily that serves to introduce the vows of the couple that follow, e.g.:

> *Priest:*
> The readings from Sts. John and Matthew emphasize two important facets of the Christian life: Love of God manifested in our love of our neighbor and a witnessing of that love that is the light of all mankind.
>
> In the vows that N. and N. will now pronounce, we will experience a concrete expression of love and witness. Let us pray that we might draw strength from the love of this couple, so that our lives might continue to bear witness to Christ who is the loving light of the world.

The couple rise and move to the center of the sanctuary space. They face each other, hold hands and recite vows that they have composed. When they have finished the priest comes forward with a tray bearing the rings.

> *Priest:*
> (blessing the rings)
> May these rings always be a sign to all men of the love and unity you have expressed today (gives each person a ring).

The couple now place rings on each other's fingers and recite either the traditional words (N., I wed you with this ring) or words that they have composed.

> *Priest:*
> (to couple)
> May your union before God and his Church be blessed
> (blessing)
> with great happiness and peace.
> Bring the light and love of Christ to all men.
> Be joyful and rejoice always in the Lord,
> and his peace will be with you always. Amen.

The bride and groom kiss; then they go into the community and give the kiss of peace to as many of the congregation as possible. There is no formal exit.

SUGGESTIONS FOR ADAPTATION

1.
The event concludes with the kiss of peace, but it can also serve as a lead into a eucharistic liturgy, in which case the bride and groom would bring up the gifts following the kiss of peace. The eucharistic liturgy would follow their presentation of the gifts. Guidelines like those set forth in Robert Hovda's *Manual of Celebration* would help to structure the liturgy from the offertory on.

2.
The first part of the event (invitations, statements and questioning ending in communal approval) can be used as a celebration for any vocation. The ceremony could conclude with a presentation of a symbol of the vocation to the person and a blessing/congratulations sending the person forth into his chosen work.

3.
The statements and biographies could be omitted from the process and a simple questioning of the couple by the priest could take place during the offertory of a liturgy. The applause response of the community would serve as an approval of the couple's vows that follow. The presentation of the wedding attire, vesting of the priest, and decoration of the sanctuary would also be omitted.

Chapter Four
Reconciliation Event

CULTURAL GROUND

Every society has a rite whereby a person or persons who have violated a rule or principle of unity in the society perform certain actions and are reinstated in the society. We are familiar with American Indian peace pipe rituals, trials, prison and rehabilitation, and various practices of penitence in religious cults. Throughout history, there have also been times when whole cultures would seek reconciliation for some wrong they had done (e.g. Old Testament covenant renewal: Exodus 32:30—33:6) and we also do this in our national mourning of a shot-down leader, our war moratoriums and our seasonal religious observances.

Like consolidation events, reconciliation rituals seek to strengthen the dedication of a culture or community to the transcendent values underpinning it. Be they secular or religious, these rituals of repentence and renewal are always signs of growth and promise.

THE TRANSCENDENT

The transcendent in the reconciliation event is perceived as a value or principle of order in a community or individual. Hence, law, customs, ethics, fraternity and peace are common manifestations of the ritual transcendent. When these begin to disappear, the strength of the culture or individual diminishes, and something must be done to rebuild the weakened structure . . . the ritual rebinding man and his actions to the transcendent value. In Christianity, the constant call to turn from sin to selflessness mandates an on-going process of ritual renewal, whereby the individual and community are constantly focused on the ideal of love presented in Christ.

STRUCTURE

The reconciliation ritual seeks to free man to undergo two experiences: the effects of his transgression *and* a renewal of dedication to the transcendent value. Therefore every reconciliation ritual must have two parts in which these experiences are developed and felt. The event is truly a celebration, for the individual in the present action of renewal experiences his past sinfulness and reconciliation as a promise for future justification. The two parts of the reconciliation event must work together to produce a deep sense of the wholeness and unity that is the core of this ritual action.

CHRISTIAN RECONCILIATION EVENT

The following event explores the themes of sin-alienation-darkness-disharmony *and* reconciliation-fellowship-light-harmony. It allows the participants to experience darkness and sin as a necessary prelude to reconciliation in Christ, the light and first-born of the new creation. The transcendent in this ritual is Christ who makes reconciliation possible by presenting our loving Father and gifting us with the Holy Spirit.

PARTICIPANTS:
Leader: a priest or member of the community.
Community seeking to renew itself to the Christian ideal.
Three Readers.

SPACE:
Ideally, this ritual should take place out-of-doors in some place that bristles with celebratory possibili-

ties: rocks by a rolling ocean, a glade by a clear lake or a deserted beach. Yet since most of us live in cities, a park, a back yard, a vaulted church or a simple room will do.

MATERIALS:
Part I:
Selected penitential psalms (e.g., 22, 55, 69, 120, 130).
Two hand-sized rocks, or two wooden blocks for each participant.
Part II:
Typed text (1 John 1:5a-8) for leader.
Three typed texts (Genesis 1:1-6; John 1:1-5; Colossians 1:15-20) for each reader.
Large candle on table or stand (stand needed only if event is indoors).
Small bells, hand xylophones or finger cymbals for all participants.

THE EVENT

Note:
The following description of the event is aimed at the leader who should familiarize himself with its dynamics so that he can direct its performance without a script.

Before the Event

Participants should gather in the pre-dawn grayness or in a space that can be darkened. Each participant should be given sheets containing the penitential psalms, two hand-sized rocks, and a bell, xylophone or cymbal.

The leader will give the following instructions:

Leader:
The event we are about to perform celebrates our individual and communal justification in Christ. It will be divided into two parts: Part I—an experience of darkness and alienation, and Part II—an experience of light and unity.

(Part I—Darkness) Station yourselves as far apart from each other as possible. Think about your own sinfulness and the sins and alienation present in the world. Look at the penitential psalms for inspiration, and focus, if you want, on passages that capture your own experience of alienation. You will not

42

read these psalms in the first part of the event.

(After a period of reflection)

I will give a signal for the event to begin (signal: either extinguishing the lights or initiating the action). You should begin to crash the rocks together while yelling out verses of the psalms, sins, evils of the world, or anything you feel in the dynamics of the action. You should not try to communicate with other participants.

This noise will go on for some time.

Leader:
(Part II—Light) When the light comes (via the leader's lighting a candle or the dawn coming) you should stop the noisemaking and begin to harmonize with each other by repeating or harmonizing with a tone that I will begin. (This tone which can be either an Ohm or simple note can be practiced briefly at this point.) Once the tone is established, put down the rocks and pick up the musical instruments. Chime them gently as a background to the harmony of the group.

You should now begin to move slowly toward the source of light (if the light source is a candle, the group should form a circle around it; if the light is the rising sun, the group should face it in a semicircle). You should continue the harmony, and as you move closer to the other participants you should make an effort to match their tone or blend with their harmony.

After the harmony and bells have gone on for some time, three simultaneous readings (cf. technique below to instruct the readers before the event) will take place. You should continue the tone and try to harmonize with the readers who themselves will be harmonizing texts. The readings will continue until the readers feel that they have established harmony: hence the same readings may be repeated several times.

When the readings conclude, stop the tone and remain silent before the light. Following this long silence will be a reading and a concluding prayer.

NOTES FOR THE LEADER

Reading Technique: Prior to the event, the leader hands each reader a sheet with a text typed on it:

Reader I:
(Genesis 1:1-6)
In the beginning, when God created the heavens and the earth, the earth was a formless wasteland, and darkness covered the abyss, while a mighty wind swept over the waters. Then God said, "Let there be light," and there was light. God saw how good the light was. God then separated light from darkness. God called the light "day" and the darkness he called "night." Thus evening came and morning followed--the first day.

Reader II:
(John 1:1-5)
In the beginning was the Word;
the Word was in God's presence,
and the Word was God.
He was present to God in the beginning.
Through him all things came into being,
and apart from him nothing came to be.

Whatever came to be in him found life,
life for the light of men.

The light shines on in darkness,
a darkness that did not overcome it.

Reader III:
(Colossians 1:15-20)
He is the image of the invisible God,
the first-born of all creatures.
In him everything in heaven
and on earth was created,
things visible and invisible,
whether thrones or dominations,
principalities or powers;
all were created through him and for him.
He is before all else that is.
In him everything continues in being. . . .

It pleased God to make absolute fullness
reside in him,
and by means of him,
to reconcile everything in his person,
both on earth and in the heavens,
making peace through the blood of his cross.

The leader should tell the readers that they will read the texts simultaneously during the second part of the event. They will read above the harmony of the group and will try to blend the texts with each other and with the tone of the participants. They may repeat the texts as often as they want, and they may also repeat key phrases. They should stop reading *only* when they sense an established harmony-- hence one may stop before the other. They should not begin to read until the group has had a long time to establish its own harmony (it might be best for the leader to determine the starting time for the readings and give a signal). The three readers *should not practice* before the event, as this reading technique derives its impact from the on-the-spot interplay of readers and community.

CONCLUSION OF THE EVENT

It is essential that the leader allow for a long period of silence following the simultaneous readings. This period, which should be at least three minutes, serves both as reflection on the movement of the event and as a lead-in to the following concluding prayer:

> *Leader:*
> (1 John 1:5a-8)
> God is light
> and no shadow or darkness can exist in him.
> If we were to say
> that we enjoyed fellowship with him
> and still went on living in darkness,
> we should both be telling and living a lie.
>
> But if we are really living in the same light
> in which he eternally exists
> then we have true fellowship with each other
> and the blood which his Son shed for us
> keeps us clean from all sin.
>
> As children of the light we are happy to say:
> Glory be to the Father. . . .
>
> *Community:*
> and to the Son, and to the Holy Spirit.
> As it was in the beginning,
> is now and ever shall be
> world without end. Amen.

Time: As is the case in all ritual action, time should be used to create a sacred dimension; hence it is best to extend the banging in Part I beyond the point of mild irritation, and it is wise to maintain the harmony of Part II for a long time to provide a transition to and an atmosphere for the simultaneous readings. Many communities who have performed this event have lost its dynamic by rushing its actions.

SUGGESTIONS FOR ADAPTATION

1.

If the event takes place near water, participants might wash or sprinkle each other during the period of harmony before the simultaneous readings.

2.

This event has been used successfully as an Ash Wednesday event. Prior to the event, participants were asked to donate one dollar for a worthy cause. During the silence these bills were brought forward and burned in a bowl. People were then invited to anoint one another with the ashes and either say the traditional formula ("Remember, man, that you are dust, and to dust you shall return"), or improvise one of their own. The anointing was followed with a period of silence and the service concluded with the prayer in the text (1 John 1:5a-8)

3.

The event has also been used as a retreat meditation on sin and redemption. When used in this manner, it is profitable to follow the event with a period of shared prayer.

4.

The transcendent in the event need not be Christian. The event has been used as a moratorium ritual, wherein lists of the war dead were used in place of the penitential psalms and secular readings on peace were substituted for the biblical texts.

5.

This event has been done without Part II (Light) as a means of tuning people in to the anger and violence within them. When used this way, it should be followed by a period of silence and concluded with an open sharing of the feelings generated by the event.

Chapter Five
Departure Event

CULTURAL GROUND

Many of us have spent hours in movie theaters or before the tube watching films about the Second World War. In most of these movies the most poignant moment was the dockside scene when wives, lovers and families stood far below the decks of a troop ship waving frantically at the men who were going off to war. As "Over There" or some equally patriotic melody played over the speaker system, the ship pulled out leaving loved ones behind and many tear-filled eyes in the audience.

This film sequence, which drew much of its impact from a fact of human existence, the departure of a loved one, is but a small star in the galaxy of the departure rituals that have been an ever present pattern in history. We need only to recall Ulysses, Christ, Thomas More, J.F.K. or the death of a loved one to realize that the departure event is very much a part of our ritual tradition and lives.

THE TRANSCENDENT

In a very real sense the transcendent or focal element in the departure event is the value or spirit of the person leaving or gone. The ritual seeks to direct individual energies and relate them to the person departing, and in doing this to somehow make each participant more aware that the person going (gone) is a real part of him. An added element is the

fact that departure is a universal which all must face; hence the event has a built-in emotional impact that is present only in the elemental rituals celebrating birth, life and death. In religious cultures, departure, usually in the form of death or pilgrimage, connotes a passage into another more profound realm of existence; thus the human transcendent of personal value becomes part of a more comprehensive value perceived as promise, reward, liberation or finality.

STRUCTURE

Our sense as cultural beings tells us what the structure of a departure event should be. A period of preparation precedes the departure ceremony, which is followed by a period when those left behind experience the absence of the person who has departed. Our experience also informs us that the division of the event is not so neatly made, for even in the preparatory and departure stages we are experiencing feelings of absence, loss or, in some instances, hope. It would be foolish to deny the presence of these feelings, for they lend power to the event and should be released and focused. The structure makes present the transcendent which provides the ground for the many emotions inherent in the departure event; this fact should become clear in the following event.

CHRISTIAN DEPARTURE EVENT

One usually wonders about the necessity of wakes and funerals, when theology and medicine affirm that the essential life force of the person is gone shortly after death, until he becomes aware of man's ritual need which bypasses biology and doctrine. Since death doesn't usually notify the ritualist of its immanence, he cannot prepare a three-part ceremony, dying-death-aftermath, to frame the actual event. He must satisfy his ritual need after the event in a sort of re-presentation of the fact which is already a deepening reality. He must create a structure that replays the person's life and death and grounds it in the higher force of hope and divine promise. He must also allow all of the feelings that death evokes to be present in the event; there should be anger or disappointment, real sorrow and hope as the purgings that are a dynamic necessity.

We have chosen a death rite, mainly because we have not experienced a structure that provides for the real, emotional dynamic that should be present in departure rituals. We feel that in many instances death rituals have become too matter of fact, too theologized and too controlled. The Lazarus

story of John 11 has been chosen as a paradigm for this event because it represents an almost perfect picture of Christian death as an individual and communal experience.

PARTICIPANTS:

The *body* (in closed or open coffin) or a symbol of the departed person, e.g., his picture.

The *family* and *friends* of the deceased.

Priest, minister or *leader.*

Five readers/speakers.

SPACE:

a living room, a church or a funeral parlor.

MATERIALS:

Text of the event for the leader.

One large candle and smaller candles for all participants.

A black draping for the coffin (if used in the Event).

A white draping for the coffin (if used in the Event).

Celebratory vestments for the leader.

THE EVENT

The Sending Forth

Mourners gather before an open or closed black-draped coffin. The lights in the church/room should be bright and there should not be flowers or candles to distract from the starkness of the coffin.

The mourners are given time to settle in their seats; then the priest/minister or leader enters (he should not be vested and should wear appropriate mourning attire).

Priest:

We have come together to celebrate the life of a wonderful and dear person, N. Let us listen carefully to these words and events from N.'s life:

1st Statement:

A personal letter or parts of a personal diary or notebook of the dead person. If a letter is used it should be read by its recipient.

2nd Statement:

An account of the good things the person did, most effectively done by one who was personally touched by the departed person's goodness. Several such accounts could be given here.

3rd Statement:

A narration of a humorous event from the departed person's life. This statement might include the telling of the person's favorite joke.

4th Statement:

A description of the most difficult problem the departed person faced in life, and the means he took to solve it.

When these readings/statements are over, there should be a long period of silence followed by these or similar words from the priest/leader.

Priest:

N. was a warm and loving man/woman who meant much to all of us here. We are very much like Martha of St. John's Gospel who had lost her brother:

Reading:

There was a certain man named Lazarus who was sick. He was from Bethany, the village of Mary and her sister Martha. (This Mary whose brother Lazarus was sick was the one who anointed the Lord with perfume and dried his feet with her hair.) The sisters sent word to Jesus to inform him, "Lord, the one you love is sick." Upon hearing this, Jesus said: "This sickness is not to end in death; rather it is for God's glory, that through it the Son of God may be glorified."

Jesus loved Martha and her sister and Lazarus very much. Yet, after hearing that Lazarus was sick, he stayed on where he was for two days more. Finally he said to his disciples, "Let us go back to Judea." "Rabbi," protested the disciples, "with the Jews only recently trying to stone you, you are going back up there again?" Jesus answered: "Are there not twelve hours of daylight? If a man goes walking by day he does not stumble because he sees the world bathed in light. But if he goes walking at night he will stumble since there is no light in him." After uttering these words, he added, "Our beloved Lazarus has fallen asleep, but I am going there to wake him." At this the disciples objected, "Lord, if he is asleep his life will be saved." Jesus had been speaking about his death, but they thought he meant sleep in the sense of slumber. Finally Jesus said plainly, "Lazarus is dead. For your sakes I am glad I was not there, that you may come to believe. In any event, let us go to him." Then Thomas (the name means "Twin") said to his fellow disciples, "Let us go along, to die with him."

When Jesus arrived at Bethany, he found that Lazarus had already been in the tomb four days The

village was not far from Jerusalem--just under two miles--and many Jewish people had come out to console Martha and Mary over their brother. When Martha heard that Jesus was coming she went to meet him, while Mary sat at home. Martha said to Jesus, "Lord if you had been here, my brother would never have died. . . ."

Priest:
(at the conclusion of the reading)
Like Martha we are angry and confused and ask the Lord to hear us.

We are saddened and even angered by N.'s death.

Community:
Lord, hear us!

Priest:
We are afraid of death, we feel sorry for ourselves, we do not enjoy loss.

Community:
Lord, hear us!

Priest:
We do not understand why N. had to die now.

Community:
Lord, hear us!

Priest:
We would like to push the clock back to another time.

Community:
Lord, hear us!

Priest:
Help us, O Lord, in the presence of death.

Community:
Lord, hear us!

The petitions are followed by a long period of silence; then the priest instructs the people to read Psalm 23 or to listen to a hymn or music which expresses hope.

While the reading or song is in progress, the coffin is closed (if necessary) and draped by two of the readers with the white cloth. The priest puts on celebratory vestments in the presence of the community. After the reading, draping and vesting, the priest addresses the community:

Priest:

The story of Lazarus does not end in anger and frustration, for in it we discover a promise to all who believe that Christ is the resurrection and the life.

Reader:

(same as above)

"Your brother will rise again," Jesus assured her. "I know he will rise again," Martha replied, "in the resurrection on the last day." Jesus told her: "I am the resurrection and the life: whoever believes in me, though he should die, will come to life; and whoever is alive and believes in me will never die. Do you believe this?" "Yes, Lord," she replied. "I have come to believe that you are the Messiah, the Son of God: he who is to come into the world."

When she had said this she went back and called her sister Mary. "The Teacher is here, asking for you," she whispered. As soon as Mary heard this, she got up and started out in his direction. (Actually Jesus had not yet come into the village but was still at the spot where Martha had met him.) The Jews who were in the house with Mary consoling her saw her get up quickly and go out, so they followed her, thinking she was going to the tomb to weep there. When Mary came to the place where Jesus was, seeing him, she fell at his feet and said to him, "Lord if you had been here my brother would never have died." When Jesus saw her weeping, and the Jews who had accompanied her also weeping, he was troubled in spirit, moved by the deepest emotions. "Where have you laid him?" he asked. "Lord, come and see," they said. Jesus began to weep, which caused the Jews to remark, "See how much he loved him!" But some said, "He opened the eyes of that blind man. Why could he not have done something to stop this man from dying?" Once again troubled in spirit, Jesus approached the tomb.

It was a cave with a stone laid across it. "Take away the stone," Jesus directed. Martha, the dead man's sister, said to him, "Lord, it has been four days now; surely there will be a stench!" Jesus replied, "Did I not assure you that if you believed you would see the glory of God displayed?" They then took away the stone and Jesus looked upward and said: "Father, I thank you for having heard me. I know that you always hear me but I have said this for the sake of

the crowd, that they may believe that you sent me."
Having said this, he called loudly, "Lazarus, come
out!" The dead man came out, bound hand and foot
with linen strips, his face wrapped in a cloth. "Untie
him," Jesus told them, "and let him go free."

This caused many of the Jews who had come to visit
Mary, and had seen what Jesus did, to put their
faith in him.

At the end of the reading, the priest places a large candle on
the coffin. The readers who draped the coffin now place
some flowers at the base of the candle.

Priest:
Our brother/sister is another Lazarus, a dear friend
of Jesus, for whom the promise of resurrection into
light is a reality. For N. believed in these words:

"I am the resurrection and the life, he who believes
in me, though he die, shall live, and whoever lives
and believes in me shall never die."

N., we are happy for your belief; we are strengthened by your faith. We rejoice, N., that you live in
the light.

The Priest now lights the large candles on the coffin and
says:

Priest:
The light of Christ shines to brighten darkness into
day. The light of belief, present in N. and his/her
life, still burns brightly in the lives of those he/she
loved. Let us come forward and share in N.'s belief
in Christ's light. Let us carry that light before us so
that all men may see and believe that in Christ
darkness and death are overcome.

The priest calls the community forward and hands each person a small candle. The person lights the small candle from
the large one on the coffin and then moves to a position
behind the coffin.

After all the candles are lit, a procession led by the coffin
carried by friends and the large candle carried by the priest
moves out of the church/room to the place of burial.

Note:
If the community should have to travel by car to the grave-
site, candles should be extinguished. The procession with
lighted candles should reform at the cemetery.

THE BURIAL

This part of the event should be very brief as it provides an AMEN to the church ceremony.

Mourners carrying lighted candles encircle the grave. The priest should bless the coffin either with holy water or by pouring wax from the large candle so that a cruciform shape is formed on the coffin lid. While this blessing is taking place, the priest says:

> *Priest:*
>
> "I am the resurrection and the life; he who believes in me, though he die, shall live, and whoever lives and believes in me shall never die."

The priest should then hold the lighted candle high and say:

Priest:

Christ is the light of the world. We believe that through him and with him and in him all praise and glory are given to you, Father, in union with the Holy Spirit today and forever.

Community:

Amen.

> The priest then hands the large candle to the family of the deceased. The family leads a procession from the grave and recites the Lord's Prayer with the doxology as they process.

CONCLUSION

The following day a liturgy of resurrection should be celebrated and the large lighted candle should be placed in a prominent place in the sanctuary. This same candle should be used at subsequent memorial Masses or services.

SUGGESTIONS FOR ADAPTATIONS

1.

This rite strives to maintain a simplicity and directness that should be present in a departure rite. There is some opportunity to vary texts and petitions, but it is important to allow the emotions of the mourners to be expressed in the Scripture, personal selections, and petitions. One must be careful not to overdo the mournful side, lest the transition into hope is made impossible.

2.

The entire service could take place on the last evening of the wake, in which case the body would be present at the Eucharist the following day. This is, however, a less satisfactory means of celebrating this event.

Chapter Six
Sharing Event

CULTURAL GROUND

Sharing events play a major role in the history of ritual, for they celebrate a basic fact: man's dependence on and fellowship with his neighbor and in most instances his God. Of the many types of sharing events found in ritual texts, the most familiar ones are the ritual meals wherein food and drink become much more than mere sustenance. We are aware of this transformation of food and drink in the many ritual meals we have experienced, so a mere mention of Thanksgiving, testimonial dinners and eucharistic banquets precludes our developing a history of ritual sharing in primitive and religious cultures. As ritual beings we have used food and drink as one of the most important symbols of caring and love: we take friends out to dine, we learn creative cookery from Julia Childs, we set splendid tables for holiday gatherings, etc., until we find ourselves expressing so much fellowship that we have to go to Weight Watchers.

THE TRANSCENDENT

In most sharing events, the operative transcendent is the value of fellowship, but in the higher ritual structures this transcendent is focused in the God who is a source of the

many blessings being celebrated. Sharing in these religious rituals extends the meaning of man giving to man, by positing God as the supreme giver in the community. Many of our current sharing events, from Christmas gift-giving to Thanksgiving, have lost the sacred dimension, yet because their ritual action is sound they still generate meaning in their symbols. We should not, as many churchmen do, lament the absence of God in these celebrations, for the lack is not merely a seasonal one. These ritual structures testify to the fact that people are celebrating what they hold valuable--eating together and enjoying the comfort and security of prosperity. For the ritualist, the fact that many cultures ritualize sharing is a positive energy which is worth encouraging by the creation of new sharing structures.

STRUCTURE

Sharing events are somewhat difficult to structurally define, as they take many forms from simple gift-giving events to complex meals. A study of many sharing rituals provides this general outline of the sharing event: a period of preparation is followed by a meeting of the participants where gifts are presented and shared in an atmosphere of joy and thanksgiving. Further analysis of the outline reveals five stages of action:

> *Preparation* of the gifts/food/drink, of the participants and of the space where the event will take place.
> *Meeting* of the participants in the prepared space.
> *Presentation* of the prepared gifts/food/drink.
> *Sharing* of the prepared gifts/food/drink.
> *Thanksgiving* for the gifts and the freedom to share them.

Reflection on the experience of a dinner party concretizes these five elements: invited guests dress up at home while the hosts are preparing the party, food and space; guests arrive and meet the hosts and other guests; food is presented and consumed and all give thanksgiving by enjoying the food, company and conversation.

SHARING EVENT

The following sharing event will be rather complex, since it strives to flesh out the five structural elements necessary for ritual sharing.

The event came about as a result of a request by the Unit-

ed Ministry of Wesleyan University, Middletown, Connecticut, to create a celebration for all members of the university community. Since the event was to take the place of the usual ecumenical Communion service, the ministers suggested that the event provide for some type of sharing but not a specifically eucharistic one, since that would tend to exclude the non-Christians who were expected to be present for the event.

The guidelines set down by the ministers created a problem as to the nature of the transcendent grounding such an event. It could not be Christian. After much thought, the concept of a university as a place where talents are shared in a process celebrating man's creativity became a focal point locating a viable transcendent--unity through shared talents.

Rather than narrate the many stages of preparation leading up to the actual event, we will allow the event to speak for itself.

PARTICIPANTS:

Organizer(s):
To arrange for place, personnel, key participants and materials for the event.

Director:
(a) To instruct technicians and key participants concerning their functions in the event.
(b) To run a brief rehearsal for all of the above prior to the event.
(c) To brief all the participants on the theme and structure immediately before the event.
(d) To keep the action of the event moving during its performance by providing cues for the key participants and, when necessary, by leading the people into a specific activity.

Readers:
Two ministers.
Ten additional readers drawn from faculty,
students and townspeople (these people who know the structure of the event also help to facilitate action in the stages of the ritual).

Musicians:
Chapel choir members and their director.
Flamenco guitarists and singers.
Medieval ensemble--recorders, guitar and percussion.
Two folk singers.

Artists:
A Javanese dancer--faculty member.
An actor--student.

Technicians:
A lighting man.
A student to run the sound system (microphones, records and tapes).

Participants:
(in addition to those listed above) Two hundred people from the university and town.

Place:
Theater 92, a converted church on the Wesleyan campus; no fixed seating (open space), fine lighting and sound systems.

MATERIALS:
General:
Record albums: Rolling Stones—"Let It Bleed"
"Sticky Fingers"
"Hot Rocks"
Carole King—"Tapestry"
James Taylor—"Mudslide Slim"
Microphones with long cables.
Colored spotlights on dimmer circuits--focused on the theater floor.

SPECIFIC:
Part I (Preparation)
White paper hospital gowns for all participants.
Balloons for all.
"Satisfaction"—Rolling Stones.

Part II (Meeting)
20 very large cardboard cartons.
3 dozen jars of poster paints.
200 plastic cups for mixing paints.
150 paint brushes.
200 sheets of assorted colored and wrapping paper.
20 rolls of streamers--assorted colors.
20 rolls of masking tape.
Texts for ten readers ad lib (cf. Event).

Part III (Presentation—also used in Part IV)
(These materials are placed on a large table on the apron of the stage)
250 plastic glasses filled with various wines.
300 flowers in large containers.

Large quantities of assorted bread--French, Rye, Bagels, Datenut, Wonder, etc.
200 pieces of assorted fruit--mainly apples, bananas and oranges.
200 sticks of incense--assorted.
50 lighted candles.

Part IV (Sharing)
Bowl of flowers for the Javanese dancer.
Texts for the two ministers (cf. Event).
Bread, wine and fruit.

Part V (Thanksgiving)
Text for the two ministers (cf. Event).
"You've Got a Friend" from "Tapestry"--Carole King and/or
"You've Got a Friend" from "Mudslide Slim"--James Taylor;
Rolling Stones--ad lib dance music from albums listed.

THE EVENT

Introduction

As the people entered Theater 92 they were welcomed by the two ministers and the director. Two of the readers handed out the white paper hospital gowns to the people and instructed them to congregate in the center of the open theater space. After all had arrived and time had been given for the participants to get accustomed to the surroundings, the director took one of the hand microphones and addressed the people:

Director:
Welcome!
The event which we will perform this evening celebrates the sharing of great creative gifts that takes place on the Wesleyan campus. We will attempt to ritualize that sharing in a five-part event that resembles an art happening. You are encouraged to improvise on the structure, to create your own sub-events or to just relax and have fun.

I will give you brief instructions before each part of the event. They will be guidelines for your own activity.

We are now ready to begin.

Part I (Preparation)

Director:

To prepare ourselves for the positive creative energies that will be released in the event, it is necessary that we get rid of all our negative feelings--anything that will prevent us from releasing positive energies.

Balloons will now be handed out. Fill them up with all your negativity and batter them around until they are smashed. When all the balloons are smashed the choir will lead us in song.

The balloons were handed out and time was given for the people to inflate them. When everybody was ready, the director gave a signal to the sound man and "Satisfaction" by the Rolling Stones blared over the sound system. The participants battered the balloons around, danced, stamped, laughed and chanted "I can't get no satisfaction . . ." with the record. When all the balloons were smashed, the choir began "Amazing Grace," an old Bible Belt hymn celebrating man's freedom from darkness and sin. As each verse progressed, ιore and more of the participants joined in until the whole group was singing strongly. The communal singing served to make an easy transition into Part II of the event which the director introduced.

Part II (Meeting)

Director:

On the left-hand side of the theater is a large pile of ugly cardboard cartons. In the front of the theater are supplies: paints, colored paper and streamers. Please join with others in decorating these boxes for the celebration of creativity that will take place later on.

The people took the boxes and broke up into small working groups. They began to mix paint, cut out paper, and plan their group design, but more importantly they talked with each other and visited other groups. Some began to paint the white paper gowns and their faces and hands. The building energy had taken over.

During the building process many planned and unplanned sub-events took place:

The medieval musicians played and wandered in and out among the working people.
The actor, an accomplished mime, entertained each of the groups.
Readers, who had been chosen for their ability in a

foreign language, read to each group:
Spanish--poems from Garcia Lorca.
French--poems from Villon.
Japanese--classical Haikus.
Greek--selections from Kazantzakis and St. Luke.

After the people had been given a long time to work on decorating the boxes, the director took the hand microphone and introduced Part III of the event.

Part III (Presentation of Gifts)

Director:

Each group and every individual has worked to transform ugly cardboard boxes into beautiful things.

We would like to build a large structure out of these boxes. Please bring them forward and join with others in building the structure.

On the stage you will find bread, wine, flowers, incense and candles. Place all of these on the structure you have built.

The people came forward and began to build a large, many-leveled structure in the center of the floor close to the edge of the stage. They began to place bread, wine, incense, candles and flowers on the structure which was transformed further by the color of the flowers, smoke and scent of the incense and the glint of the wine in plastic cups. When the structure was complete, the director took the microphone and spoke.

Part IV (Sharing)

Director:

Please form a large open horseshoe space in front of the structure (he gives a signal to sit down when the space has been formed). We will now praise our creativity and the creative powers of all men.

Follow the lead of the choir.

The choir began a chromatic triad and established a simple harmony which the people could join. In a short while, a beautiful, peaceful sound came from the group. The two ministers stepped into the center of the open space and spoke these words over the harmony of the people:

Minister I: We praise and celebrate man's creation.

Minister II: For . . . Let it Bleed, Tapestry, American Beauty, Mudslide Slim and Bangladesh.

Minister I: For: Miss American Pie, George Jackson and J. T.

Minister II: For . . . Clockwork Orange, Clare's Knee, Straw Dogs, Carnal Knowledge and The French Connection.

Minister I: For: Stanley, Eric, Mike and Sam.

Minister II: For . . . The Female Eunuch, Prisoner of Sex, and The Feminine Mystique.

Minister I: For: Germaine, Kate and Norman.

Minister II: For . . . Do It, Without Jesus or Marx, No Bars to Manhood, and Soul on Ice.

Minister I: For: Jerry, Daniel, Jean and Eldridge.

Minister II: For . . . Guernica, Christina's World, Marilyn and Broadway Boogie

Minister I: For: Pablo, Andrew, Piet and Andy.

Minister II: For all of us who are creators.

Minister I: For artists, writers, musicians and parents.

Minister II: For jocks, protesters and craftsmen.

Minister I: For poets, priests and prophets.

Minister II: For farmers, masons and plumbers.

Minister I: For cooks, dancers and actors.

Minister II: For teachers, mystics and magicians.

Minister I: For everyone who chooses to build rather than destroy.

Minister II: We give thanks and praise.

Note:
This text should be changed to make its references more current.
The harmony died out at the end of the readings. Then a series of performances blessing and celebrating man's creativity took place:
1.
The flamenco guitarists and singers entertained the group and led them in song and rhythmic clapping.

2.
An actor stood up and read Psalm 8 and the speech "What a piece of work is man" from Hamlet (Act II, Scene ii).
3.
Two folk singers entertained the group and led them in song.
4.
A chemistry professor from India chanted a Buddhist hymn of praise and thanksgiving.
5.
The Javanese dancer performed a Balinese temple dance and scattered flower petals on the structure and on the seated people.

After the performances celebrating man's creativity, the two ministers stepped forward and read the following prayer:

> *Minister I:* Yes is touching.
>
> *Minister II:* Yes is seeing faces and light.
>
> *Minister I:* Yes is smelling flowers, bodies and incense.
>
> *Minister II:* Yes is tasting wine and bread.
>
> *Minister I:* Yes is body and blood--bones and flesh.
>
> *Minister II:* Yes is life and death--love and separation.
>
> *Minister I:* Yes is now and always--sometimes and forever.
>
> *Minister II:* Yes is O.K. and Amen--all right and right on.
>
> *Minister I:* Yes is Yahweh, Jesus Christ, Buddha, me and you.
>
> *Minister II:* Yes is everything now.

At the conclusion of the prayer, the director took the mike and gave the following instructions to the people:

> *Director:*
> Would you now take the bread, wine and fruit and, in the spirit of the sharing that has taken place tonight, feed one another?

The people moved to the structure and began to feed one another. This movement brought many more of the people into contact with one another. When the sharing of the food was over, one of the ministers took the hand microphone and addressed the group:

Part V (Thanksgiving)

> *Minister I:*
> We celebrate and bless what we have done tonight.
> We praise the burst balloons and the Rolling Stones.
> We praise our song and dance.
> We praise our painting, costumes and clowning.
> We praise the wine in plastic cups.
> We praise the Wonder Bread and bagels.
> We praise apples, bananas and oranges.
> We praise incense from India and flowers from the greenhouse.
> We praise this time.
> We bless this space.
> We bless and praise one another.

At the conclusion of the prayer the minister asked everybody to form a large circle and join in a round dance. "You've Got a Friend" by Carole King was played over the sound system and the people began to move and invent their own dance. At the conclusion of the King song, "Let Us Bleed" by the Rolling Stones was played and the dancing picked up in tempo. At this point the sound man took over and played selections at random, and the group responded by dancing in groups rather than as individuals or couples. The event ended in this dance of thanksgiving.

Epilogue: When the music was over, the people spontaneously began to clean up the theater space. This cleaning up was an added thanks directed to the United Ministry who had sponsored the event.

SUGGESTIONS FOR ADAPTATION

1.

The entire Wesleyan event could be adapted and made into a Christian Eucharist. The unifying transcendent would be Christ, calling all to share the gifts of creation in praise and thanksgiving to the Father, the source of these gifts. The following guidelines should help in this adaptation:

(a)

Part I (Preparation): The Reconciliation Event of the previous chapter could be used in its entirety as a preparatory rite, since it moves from negativity to a focusing of positive energies in the redemptive activity of Christ.

(b)

Part II (Meeting): People could be called to construct an altar out of the cardboard boxes and colored paper. A text like Romans 8:18 ff. could be used

as a reminder to the people of their creative duties as Christians. A Gospel text like the Beatitudes, Luke 6:17 ff., might be read and developed, stressing the idea of the Christian's responsibility to share with all men.

(c)

Part III (Presentation of Gifts): Besides building the altar, the community could sing Paul Quinlan's version of Psalm 122 ("How I rejoiced when I heard I was going to go to the house of the Lord . . .") as they place bread, wine, flowers and incense on the altar (fruit would be omitted). The celebrant would pray offertory prayers over the gifts, e.g.:

We pray that these wines become the one blood that redeems us from sin and promises us life everlasting.

A triadic harmony like the one used in the Wesleyan event could be used as a grounding over which a canon (Eucharistic Prayer IV or another on the theme of creation) would be prayed or chanted.

(d)

Part IV (Sharing): This part could open with the Lord's Prayer as a table blessing and continue with the community feeding one another from the altar.

(e)

Part V (Thanksgiving): At this time a series of bidding prayers would be most effective. They should stress Thanksgiving—for example:

Celebrant:

For the gift of creation and the power to transform the world,

Community:

We are thankful, O Lord.

Celebrant:

For the many breads and many wines that have become the one body and blood of Jesus Christ,

Community:

We are thankful, O Lord.

Individuals from the community should be invited to make up their own prayers of thanksgiving. The event would conclude with a blessing by the celebrant.

2.

Parts of the event can be used for creating single events:

(a)

The balloon activity can, with the addition of texts like John 3:1-21, be used as a penance rite.

(b)
The building of a structure out of boxes which have been transformed by groups is a good way of uniting people. This activity has been used in a New York City welfare hotel as a means of breaking down the structure of alienation caused by the architecture of the building and the sorry condition of its inhabitants. In this case the boxes formed a table from which refreshments were served.

Conclusion:
From Performer to Creator

Harold Pinter, one of the world's most creative and successful playwrights, spent the years before his playwriting career began as an actor in British repertory and touring companies. One day, a friend of his in the drama department of England's Bristol University, who was intrigued by an idea for a play that Pinter had sketched for him in a past meeting, wrote to him and requested a script within a week's time. Years later in a BBC interview with Kenneth Tynan, the now successful playwright reflected on this challenge to move from performance to writing: "I wrote back to him and told him to forget about the whole thing. And then I sat down and wrote it in four days. I don't quite know how it happened, but it did." The four-day venture in 1957 produced "The Room," a highly inventive play that is still fascinating audiences throughout the world.

The movement from Harold Pinter, actor-performer, to Harold Pinter, playwright-creator, parallels the movement from participant-performer to maker-creator in ritual. It is unlikely that Pinter could have written the engaging structure of "The Room" or its exciting language without his years of experience performing the plays of proven artists. It is not unlikely that you, who have gained spiritual experience and knowledge from the performance of this book's six scripts and from other ritual activities, are now ready to move from ritual participant to ritual maker.

The person undertaking the creation of a ritual event must prepare himself by reflecting on the dynamics that are always present in successful and effective ritual. His most convenient method of preparation is a process of evaluation whereby he examines past ritual experience and in so doing stimulates the ritual senses that must be operating before the creation of an event. By evaluating all ritual experiences, the individual acquires the knowledge that makes the process of ritual-making an exciting and liberating experience.

THE RITUAL SENSES

Time

Ritual should bring participants into a new dimension of time where deeper realities can be experienced. As regards religious ritual, this dimension has been called *sacred* (Mir-

cea Eliade, *The Sacred and Profane*), but in more experiential language this dimension is known as *timelessness*.

Part I of the Reconciliation Event (Chapter IV) sought to provide this timeless dimension by having the participants in the ritual bang hand-size rocks together and shout out psalms and world evils. In extending this physical activity to an extreme, participants eventually lose their self-consciousness and are taken up by an activity which frees them to experience their own alienation, disharmony and sinfulness. Even if the individual were to stop banging and shouting, as is often the case in this event, he could not escape the environment of noise that envelops him. The extension of an activity to the point of frustration, anger, and no escape creates a dimension of time that frees man to experience his own alienation and that of others on a level of reality that exceeds the depth of ordinary experience.

If one looks at the Sunday service schedules of most churches, he discovers that sacred time has been replaced by programmed time. Events taking place within these narrow confines rarely enter the timelessness that frees one to have a deep communal and individual experience of God. In most churches the great truth "Love is time" does not apply.

> *Does the ritual lead participants into the dimension of timelessness and free them from the standard getting-the-job-done time that characterizes most human experience?*

Action

Ritual action, which is grounded in the way man enbodies— symbolizes his relation to a transcendent, is a deeply personal and communal action which reveals man to himself, man to the transcendent and man to others. In the words, gestures and movements that comprise ritual action, man acts on a level that exceeds everydayness. His action, which is rooted in his belief/faith and which is expressed in symbolism, is truly sacred.

The Initiation Event of Chapter I sought to contrast everydayness and sacredness. The participant seeking initiation into mature Christianity is invited to symbolize in word and gesture his faith and trust in God. He must choose to leave the world of playfulness and the security of its easy escape. He must choose to reveal his trust and belief in himself and God, and by his actions draw others into that belief. In the actions of this ritual, all participants experience a level of reality that is set apart from the ordinary. Their action which is grounded in their belief becomes sacred.

Ideally, the credal formulae of religions should be sacred actions. They should possess the same energy that is present in the personal choice of both the initiation and commitment rites. Their action should embody and reveal individual and communal belief, for they contain exciting dynamics that could make their action sacred. The ritual-maker must address the following question to credal formulae, offertories, prayers of consecration, blessings and other existing actions, not to destroy them but to sacralize them:

> *Does ritual action become sacred and revelatory or is it characterized by elements of everydayness, routineness, impersonalism, security or obligation?*

Space

Ritual space, like time and action, should be a liberating element which allows participants to experience a deeper reality of existence. It should not confine or alienate unless those experiences are being celebrated; it should always stand ready to be shaped and constituted sacred by the actions of the people.

In the Sharing Event (Chapter V) an open space became many things through the actions of the participants in the ritual. The transformation of space from ordinary to sacred in this event parallels the Hopi Shaman's transformation of bare earth into a sand painting possessing great power or the priest and soldiers making a piece of the battlefield a church. In its capacity to freely respond to man's ritual needs, space is made holy.

Most of our churches are performance spaces. Their ranks of seats facing sanctuary areas resemble theaters. Their organization of space allows only a limited range of action that sets up an audience-performer relationship. Our churches do not lend themselves to the participation called for in contemporary liturgical reform.

This question seeks to sensitize the ritual-maker to the importance of space:

> *Is a space flexible enough to be constituted sacred by the actions and belief of the participants in a ritual or does it dominate and allow only limited "sacred" action?*

Structure

Every successful ritual event must maintain throughout its structure a tension between freedom and control.

Freedom in a ritual structure comes about by an arrangement of time, action and space that allows each participant to experience and express his own feelings and belief. The

readings and statements of the Departure Event (Chapter VI) seek to provide a loose framework within which individual mourners can experience their own loss. Freedom in ritual allows man to express belief and emotion that would remain unexpressed in routine activity, and that expression frees man to perceive himself in a new, and often deeper, way.

Control in ritual provides direction for the individual energies of the participants. It arises only when the transcendent ground of the ritual is clear, for it is the transcendent that unifies the action in ritual. For example, the departure ritual would not have unity if individual emotions were not led through the transitional petitions to a grounding in Christ's promise in the gospel story of Lazarus. Control through the transcendent also provides for the communal aspect of ritual, for it unifies the individual actions of the participants by positing a common ground or belief.

We stated that ritual maintains the tension between freedom and control; this requires some explanation. If for example you were to serve countless cocktails to the participants before the reconciliation event, and then hand them sticks and rocks and tell them to express their anger, you might have a riot on your hands. If you took the same group of people, omitted the cocktails, stationed them in fixed positions, selected one verse from the psalms for them to shout, and practiced them in a cadenced beating of the rocks, you would have a study in boredom.

In 1972 the freewheeling Democratic and programmed Republican conventions clearly demonstrated that their ritual-makers did not ask this question:

> *Does the ritual structure provide a release and focus of individual and communal energies?*

RITUAL-MAKING

Once the ritual senses--time, action, space and structure-- have been activated, the movement to the creation of a ritual event is quite easy. Now, the only question that must be asked is this: What do I (we) want to celebrate? Answers leap out from everywhere: newspaper stories, significant events, strong feelings, deep concerns, unfulfilled religious needs or merely the desire to have a party. You are surrounded by celebratory possibilities and must make a choice.

Suppose you have just finished an article on the American tax system in the *New York Times Magazine* section and

you are angry. Its details deepen your concern about the widening gap between the rich and poor in America. You live in a middle-income neighborhood where taxes hit the hardest, yet you feel that you and your neighbors are not addressing the problem of economic injustice. You believe that something can be done to encourage the people to take action to prevent the gap from widening further. You decide to create an event which will sensitize the people in your area, and you are able to enlist the help of some of your friends. You get permission from a local church to use any of their spaces and set a date for the event.

One evening you sit down with your friends and begin planning the event. Since you have ritual experience, you will serve as leader/organizer of the group's creative process.

The following description of a process of group ritual-making takes the liberty of condensing many meetings into one. We trust that the reader will allow us this fiction.

After a long discussion period developing the ideas of the *Times* article and extending them to include other experiences of economic injustice, the group discovers that there are several organizations and individuals in the community working to offset this injustice. The group decides that it would like to create an event that would sensitize the whole community to the problem and motivate them to join with those actively working to remedy the situation.

A consolidation ritual is in the making. Its focus is the right of equality, its method is action addressed to that end.

As leader, you either describe the Consolidation Ritual of Chapter IV or lead the group in a run-through of its action. They uncover its dynamics: man's obligation to direct creation (the transcendent) and the presentation and destruction of gifts (the action sensitizing people to their obligation). The group decides to use that event as a paradigm of the ritual they are creating, and some creative energies are activated.

How does one make the idea of the equal right to share wealth present as a transcendent? A group member suggests that the idea is contained in the "Bill of Rights." The group likes the text but argues from the experience of the Consolidation Ritual that if a reading is used it must be supported by an action. You suggest that some sort of action involving the equal sharing of gifts/wealth might be effective support for the text. A group member asks if there is some way in which participants might experience their equality. You recall the white hospital gowns of the Sharing Event (Chapter V) and suggest that participants dressed in these would be

symbolically equal. The group's response is favorable and a member inserts an additional idea: paint red, white and blue stripes on every gown to strengthen their symbolism. The group laughs, but then decides that the stripes are a good idea. They are satisfied with the text and gowns as statements of shared equality, but you push them further to make the sharing more dramatic. Someone asks "How about food?" and the group plays with that idea until it is decided that each participant will bring food or a beverage to be shared in the event.

At this point you assume leadership and restate what has gone on in the group process: the transcendent of man's equality is rather clearly stated by the text, gowns and shared food, yet the group has not come to a point where people experience their real inequality. You suggest that they develop and dramatize the inequality.

A group member picks up your lead and presents a working concept: participants should work for something and then have it taken away. You push him by asking him to make this concrete. He does not know how to do it, so another comes to his aid and asks if it would be too much to have participants move through a maze or labyrinth to get food. The group consensus is that maze-running is fine for rats, but not for the participants in this event. They decide that the food the people bring to the event represents work in both the purchasing and the preparation of it. If the food were to be brought for the whole group to share and, if fact, was only shared by a few, the dramatization of injustice would be present. But how could this be done?

A sort of offertory procession idea begins to be developed: each person will present his offering to the community and say a few words about the value of sharing. After his statement the person will place the offering on a large community table. The presentation and placing of food will strengthen the concept of unity through sharing.

You agree with the group that the offering is a fine idea but remind them that they must find a way in which only a few can share the offerings. This reminder stops the group for a moment; then someone suggests that the event be conducted by leader types who will share the food. The idea is good and several ideas follow: these leaders will do all the talking about equality, they will be dressed like the people, one will give a speech of welcome, one will read the "Bill of Rights," one will recite the "Give me your tired, your poor, your hungry masses . . ." poem printed on the Statue of Liberty, one will lead the group in singing "America the Beautiful" or a similar song, and then after the offerings, the

leaders will thank the people, begin the singing of "This Land Is Your Land," and once the song takes hold they will take off their gowns and carry off armfuls of the food. Someone remarks that the event couldn't end on that note, and suggests that the lights dim to darkness as the food is being taken away. He adds that when the room is in total darkness, slides depicting the poor and needy of American be shown on a screen that could have served as a backdrop behind the leaders. Another group member adds that, following the slide presentation, people from the community who are working to remedy the sort of injustice dramatized by the event step forward and make an appeal to the people to join with them in their work.

At this point, the ritual has moved from abstract idea to concrete proposals and a definite structure. A sketch of the event this group process might have produced follows.

Note:
Before the event, fliers and announcements invite the community to the brotherhood event. Each individual or family is asked to bring food and beverages to share with the other participants.

> *PARTICIPANTS:*
> Master of ceremonies
> Four readers
> Leader of song
> Organist or pianist
> Flag bearer
> Two individuals to pass out garments
> A projectionist (slides)
> Leader and workers representing community activities
> A community
> *PLACE:*
> a large room with a raised platform containing seats for the master of ceremonies, readers and song leader. Seats arranged in rows for the community.
> *MATERIALS:*
> White paper hospital gowns for all, uniformly painted with red, white and blue stripes.
> Texts of "America the Beautiful," "God Bless America," and "This Land Is Your Land" placed on all seats.
> Texts for readers.

A large table on the raised platform.
An American flag and holder for it on the platform.
Slide projector and screen serving as a backdrop behind the raised platform.
Two sets of slides: one depicting the wealth and beauty of America, one depicting America's poverty.

ACTION OF THE EVENT

As people enter the room, two individuals hand each person a hospital gown, instruct him to keep his offering with him and direct him to the seating area.

When all are seated, the song leader steps forward, signals for the audience to rise, and asks them to sing "America the Beautiful." The lights dim slightly and a procession of the master of ceremonies, readers and flag bearer enters through the singing community. They move to their positions on the platform; the flag is placed in its stand. When the verses of the song have concluded the auditorium goes dark except for a light at the piano/organ. The organist continues "America the Beautiful" as slides depicting America's beauty, brotherhood and promise are flashed on the backdrop screen. The white gowns of the master of ceremonies, etc., will reflect the color of the slides, so they should remain in their positions.

When the slides and music are over, the lights come up and the master of ceremonies signals for the people to sit and addresses them:

> *M.C.:*
> (ad lib welcome, e.g.)
> On behalf of the Community Action Committee I would like to welcome you to this ceremony celebrating the equality we all share as Americans. The theme of the event which was set in the singing and slide show will continue with some familiar readings. Please listen.
>
> *1st Reader:*
> "Bill of Rights," possibly introduced by a brief statement concerning the founding principles of America.
>
> *2nd Reader:*
> "Give me your tired, your poor . . ." poem inscribed on the base of the Statue of Liberty.
>
> *3rd Reader:*
> Walt Whitman's "I Hear America Singing."

4th Reader:
Excerpts from John F. Kennedy's inaugural address, leading up to the familiar "Ask not what your country can do for you. . . ."

When the readers have finished the master of ceremonies steps forward and addresses the people:

M.C.:
Each of you has brought an offering to share with the community gathered here tonight. In so doing you have made a concrete statement concerning the great spirit we are celebrating this evening.

I now invite each of you to come forward with your offering. I would ask, when you come up on the platform, that you turn to your brothers and sisters and offer in word or gesture the food you have brought to be shared.

After your offering place the food or beverage on the community table and return to your seat.

The individuals who handed out the garments control the flow of offerings by calling people row by row.

When the offering is over the master of ceremonies steps forward and addresses the people:

M.C.:
Thank you for your offerings. They have strengthened our sense of brotherhood and have reflected the great spirit that we are celebrating tonight. As a preparation for the sharing that will soon take place, please sing "This Land Is Your Land."

The song leader steps forward and starts the song.

When the song has gotten underway, the lights begin to dim and the slide projector goes on. The technique for the slides is this: they will begin with some of the scenes from the first presentation: then slides showing poverty and ugliness will suddenly appear in between two beautiful slides. Gradually the beautiful slides will disappear and the ugliness will take over.

The song leader will keep the people singing. The song should grow in tempo and volume.

When the first slide portraying ugliness in America flashes on the screen, the master of ceremonies, readers and flag bearer tear off their white garments and begin to gather up armfuls of food which they carry off behind the backdrop. The lights are continuously dimming and the slides are flashing as this process of stripping the table goes on.

When the table is stripped, the master of ceremonies and readers leave the stage, the organ/piano stops abruptly, the leader and accompaniest leave, and only the slides remain flashing. In time the slide projector is turned off and the community is left in total darkness.

After a long period of darkness the lights are abruptly switched on to their brightest intensity revealing a new set of people on the platform. The leader of this group (of community workers) steps forward and addresses the people:

Leader:

On behalf of the Community Action Committee, I would like to welcome you to this ceremony celebrating the inequality we all share as Americans.

What you have just experienced goes on in your lives and the lives of millions of Americans every day. Most people work very hard for food and housing; they trust in the words of the "Bill of Rights"; yet many find the pursuit of happiness to be a quest for survival.

These people on the stage with me are working to remedy some of the injustices existing in the American economic system. Like you they do not wish to destroy America. Like you they have heard John Kennedy's words: "Ask not what your country can do for you but rather what you can do for your country." They are actively responding to Kennedy's challenge and they need your help.

The readings from the "Bill of Rights," the Statue of Liberty and Whitman were familiar to you. What these people will tell you represents another voice of America. Please listen to them.

Note:

The following appeals are only suggestions. In the actual event the appeals will be determined by the type of activities going on in the community.

1st Appeal:

This person will address the group on the problem of tax laws in America, citing facts and relating what he and others are doing to remedy the situation. He will invite the interested and concerned members of the community to meet him after the appeals at one of the tables set up on the side of the room.

2nd Appeal:

This representative might focus on the Job Corps

and ask for volunteer teachers or recruiters of students. He too will invite the people to meet with him after the appeals are over.

3rd Appeal:

This one could come from a VISTA representative who will outline problems and programs going on in America. He would give the same invitation as others.

4th Appeal:

This appeal might come from a disabled war veteran who will seek the aid of the people in locating jobs for other disabled veterans, with the same invitation following.

After the appeals have been made, the leader steps forward and addresses the community:

Leader:

Thank you for listening to these people from your community. We hope that you will respond to their call for help.

The food you have brought will now be returned to the platform. We ask that you share it with your brothers and sisters in a new and perhaps deeper sense of unity.

Thank you for coming this evening.

The original group (master of ceremonies, readers, etc.) brings out the food and personally offers it to the community. The event concludes with a communal sharing, and people meeting the individuals who made the appeals.

Unlike the other events in this book, the preceding one has never been performed. It is presented in this manner for many reasons: to show the product of a hypothetical ritual-making process, to provide the reader and his community with an opportunity to perform, evaluate and adapt or reject an untried event, and, finally, to ask the reader a two-phased question: *Is this event ritual or theater, sacred or profane?*

EPILOGUE

The name Percy Bysshe Shelley usually provokes snickers in a high school class. His poetry, which is seldom taught well, often draws groans out of the same group. For most adults, Shelley's name and poetry recall classroom drudgery. Even the new romantics whose dress and life style mirror the poet's find him out of joint with the now generation.

Yet one line from the pen of this exuberant artist rings so true in our disposable, on-the-road culture. In "Ode to the West Wind," Shelley makes a statement about his poetic imagination and expression that we believe is the only apt conclusion to this book:

> Drive my dead thoughts over the universe
> Like withered leaves to quicken a new birth!

folio benjamin

folio benjamin

L'AUTEUR

Roald Dahl est né au pays de Galles, en 1916, de parents fortunés d'origine norvégienne. Avide d'aventures, il part pour l'Afrique à 18 ans et travaille dans une compagnie pétrolière, avant de devenir pilote à la Royal Air Force, pendant la Seconde Guerre mondiale. Il échappe de peu à la mort, son appareil s'étant écrasé au sol ! À la suite de cet accident, Roald Dahl se met à écrire… mais c'est seulement en 1961, après avoir publié pendant quinze ans des livres pour les adultes, que Roald Dahl devient écrivain pour la jeunesse avec *James et la Grosse Pêche*. D'autres chefs-d'œuvre ne tardent pas à suivre parmi lesquels *Charlie et la Chocolaterie*, *Le Bon Gros Géant*, *Fantastique Maître Renard*… Ses livres ont été traduits dans plus de trente-cinq langues. Depuis sa mort, en novembre 1990, Felicity, sa femme, gère la fondation Roald Dahl, qui se consacre à des causes chères à l'écrivain : la neurologie, la dyslexie, l'illettrisme et l'encouragement à la lecture, d'ailleurs l'un des thèmes essentiels de *Matilda*, son dernier roman, paru en 1988.

L'ILLUSTRATEUR

Né en 1932, en Angleterre, **Quentin Blake** publie son premier dessin à l'âge de 16 ans dans le célèbre magazine satirique *Punch*. En 1960, sort son premier livre pour enfants, en tandem avec John Yeoman. Sa collaboration avec Roald Dahl commence en 1978, année de la création de *L'Énorme Crocodile*. Ensemble, ils donneront vie à *Matilda*, *Les Deux Gredins*, *Le Bon Gros Géant*… Quentin Blake écrit et dessine aussi ses propres histoires : *Armeline Fourchedrue*, *Les Cacatoès*, *Clown*, *Le Bateau vert* et tant d'autres. Son œuvre comporte plus de 200 ouvrages d'une variété extraordinaire. Figure emblématique de l'illustration dans le monde entier, admiré par des générations d'illustrateurs, ancien directeur du *Royal College of Art*, il est devenu, en 1999, le premier Ambassadeur-Lauréat du livre pour enfants. Quentin Blake partage sa vie entre Londres et sa maison de l'Ouest de la France. En 2002, honoré du grade de chevalier des Arts et Lettres, il a également reçu le prix Andersen, « prix Nobel » du livre de jeunesse.

Fin

l'Énorme Crocodile fonce dans le soleil,
tête la première… dans le soleil brûlant !!!…
C'est ainsi qu'il grilla comme une saucisse !!!

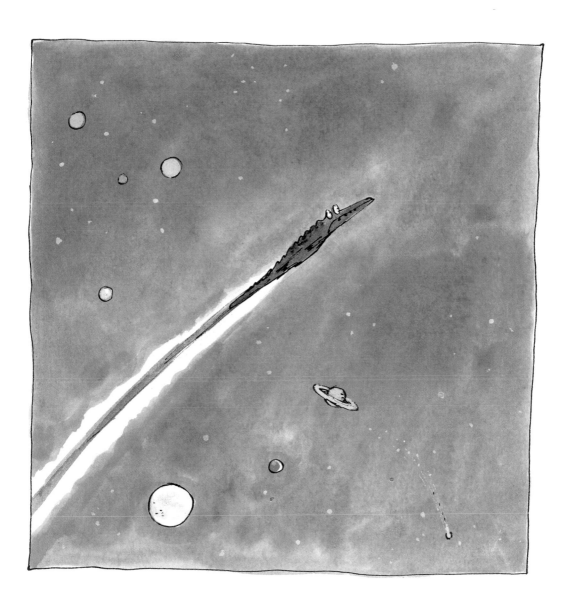

Il passait en sifflant…
whizz… dans l'espace
whizz… il dépassa la lune…
whizz… il dépassa les étoiles et les planètes…
whizz… jusqu'à ce que, enfin…
dans le plus retentissant bang !!…

Soudain, Trompette lâcha la queue du crocodile
qui partit dans le ciel comme une grosse fusée
verte. Haut dans le ciel… de plus en plus haut…
de plus en plus vite…
Il alla si vite et si haut que la terre ne fut plus
qu'un tout petit point en dessous.

Toujours plus vite…
On ne vit bientôt plus de l'Énorme Crocodile
qu'une forme tourbillonnante au-dessus de la tête
de Trompette.

Trompette fit tourner le crocodile dans
les airs. D'abord lentement. Puis plus vite…
Plus vite…
De plus en plus vite…

Trompette fila droit sur l'Énorme Crocodile
et, rapide comme l'éclair, il enroula sa trompe
autour de la queue de celui-ci, et le tint suspendu
en l'air.
– Aïe, aïe, aïe ! lâche-moi ! gémit l'Énorme
Crocodile, la tête en bas, lâche-moi ! lâche-moi !
– Non ! rétorqua Trompette, je ne te lâcherai pas !
On en a vraiment plein le dos
de tes pièges subtils !

C'est alors qu'une grosse voix profonde retentit
dans la jungle :
– Arrière, les enfants ! arrière ! arrière !
Les enfants, saisis, scrutèrent l'endroit d'où
provenait la voix. Dans un craquement de branches,
Trompette, l'éléphant, surgit hors de la jungle.
– Ce n'est pas sur un banc que vous alliez vous
asseoir, barrit-il, c'est sur l'Énorme Crocodile
qui veut vous manger !

Puis il prit lui-même la place du banc. En rentrant
la tête dans les épaules et en dissimulant sa queue,
il finit par ressembler exactement à un long banc
de bois.
Bientôt, arrivèrent deux garçons et deux filles
qui portaient des paniers remplis de victuailles.
Ils appartenaient tous à la même famille
et leur mère leur avait donné la permission
d'aller pique-niquer ensemble.
– Quelle table on prend ?
– Celle avec des fleurs !

L'Énorme Crocodile se fait aussi discret
qu'une souris. « Je vais tous les manger ! se dit-il.
Ils vont venir s'asseoir sur mon dos, je sortirai
alors brusquement la tête et je n'en ferai
qu'une bouchée croustillante et savoureuse. »

Il cueillit une belle brassée de fleurs qu'il plaça
sur une table. Il ôta un des bancs de cette même
table et le cacha derrière un buisson.

Même l'homme qui surveillait le manège
quitta son poste et s'enfuit au plus vite.
L'Énorme Crocodile, maudissant Dodu-
de-la-Plume, se replia vers les buissons pour
s'y cacher. « Qu'est-ce que j'ai faim ! je pourrais
manger six enfants avant d'être rassasié ! »

Aux alentours immédiats de la ville, il y avait
un joli petit champ entouré d'arbres et
de buissons : au lieu-dit du « Pique-Nique ».
On y avait disposé des tables et de grands bancs
en bois, et les gens pouvaient venir s'y installer
à tout moment. L'Énorme Crocodile se glissa
jusqu'à ce champ. Personne en vue !
« Et maintenant, passons au piège subtil n° 4 »,
marmonna-t-il entre ses dents.

Alors il y eut un froissement d'ailes : « flip-flap »,
et quelque chose descendit du ciel dans
un bruissement de plumes chamarrées,
c'était Dodu-de-la-Plume, l'oiseau.
Il voleta autour du manège, chantant :
– Attention, Jill ! attention ! attention ! ne monte
pas sur ce crocodile !
Jill s'immobilisa et leva les yeux.
– Ce n'est pas un crocodile en bois ! continua
Dodu-de-la-Plume. C'est un vrai. C'est l'Énorme
Crocodile de la rivière qui veut te manger !
Jill fit demi-tour et s'enfuit. Et tous les enfants
s'enfuirent.

« Passons au piège subtil n° 3 ! » susurra
l'Énorme Crocodile en se léchant les babines.

Profitant d'un moment d'inattention, il grimpa
sur le manège et s'installa entre un lion et un
dragon effroyable. Les pattes arrière légèrement
fléchies, il se tint parfaitement immobile.
On aurait dit un vrai crocodile de manège.
Bientôt de nombreux enfants envahirent
la fête. Plusieurs coururent vers le manège.
Ils étaient très excités.
– Je prends le dragon !
– Et moi, ce joli petit cheval blanc !
– À moi le lion ! »

Mais une petite fille, nommée Jill :
– Je veux monter sur ce drôle de crocodile
en bois !
L'Énorme Crocodile ne bouge pas d'une écaille,
mais il peut apercevoir la petite fille se diriger
vers lui : « Miam, miam, miam… je ne vais en faire
qu'une bouchée. »

Ce fut une belle panique parmi les enfants qui détalèrent. Jojo-la-Malice disparut dans la jungle et l'Énorme Crocodile se retrouva tout seul.

Maudissant le singe, il se replia vers les buissons pour se cacher. « J'ai de plus en plus faim ! gémit-il, c'est au moins quatre enfants que je devrai engloutir avant d'être rassasié ! »

L'Énorme Crocodile rôda aux limites de la ville, prenant grand soin de ne pas se faire remarquer. C'est ainsi qu'il arriva aux alentours d'une place où l'on achevait d'installer une fête foraine. Il y avait là des patinoires, des balançoires, des autos tamponneuses ; on vendait du pop-corn et de la barbe à papa. Il y avait aussi un grand manège. Le grand manège possédait de ces merveilleuses créatures en bois que les enfants enfourchent : des chevaux blancs, des lions, des tigres, des sirènes et leur queue de poisson, et des dragons effroyables aux langues rouges dardées.

Mais une petite fille, plus âgée que les autres,
s'étonna :
– Elle me paraît bien noueuse, cette balançoire,
non ? vous croyez qu'on peut s'y asseoir sans
danger ?
– Mais oui ! reprirent les autres en chœur.
C'est du solide !
L'Énorme Crocodile entrouvre un œil et observe
les enfants qui se pressent autour de lui.
« Bientôt, pense-t-il, l'un d'eux va prendre place
sur ma tête, alors… un coup de reins, un coup
de dent, et… miam, miam, miam ! »

À cet instant précis, il y eut un éclair brun
et quelque chose traversa le terrain de jeux,
puis bondit au sommet d'un portique.
C'était Jojo-la-Malice, le singe.
– Filez ! hurla-t-il aux enfants. Allez, filez tous !
filez, filez, filez ! ce n'est pas une balançoire,
c'est l'Énorme Crocodile qui veut vous manger !

Pour le moment, il n'y avait pas d'enfants.
Ils étaient tous à l'école. L'Énorme Crocodile
découvrit un grand morceau de bois ; le plaçant
au milieu du terrain, il s'y étendit en travers
et replia ses pattes. Il ressemblait presque, ainsi,
à une balançoire !
À l'heure de la sortie, tous les enfants
se précipitèrent vers le terrain de jeux.
– Oh regardez ! crièrent-ils, on a une nouvelle
balançoire !
Ils l'entourèrent avec des cris de joie.
– C'est moi le premier !
– Je prends l'autre bout !
– À moi d'abord !
– Non, à moi, à moi !

Julien et Marie s'enfuirent vers la ville
aussi vite qu'ils le purent.

Mais les crocodiles ont la peau dure.
Il est difficile, même à un hippopotame,
de les blesser. L'Énorme Crocodile reprit
ses esprits et rampa vers un terrain de jeux
réservé aux enfants.
« Maintenant, passons au piège subtil n° 2,
se dit-il. Celui-là fonctionnera, c'est sûr ! »

Soudain, il y eut un fracas de tonnerre !
C'était Double-Croupe, l'hippopotame.
Crachant et soufflant, il sortit de la jungle.
Tête baissée, il arrivait à fond de train !
– Attention, Julien ! hurla Double-Croupe.
Attention, Marie ! ce n'est pas un cocotier !
c'est l'Énorme Crocodile qui veut vous manger !

Double-Croupe chargea droit sur l'Énorme
Crocodile. Il le frappa de sa tête puissante
et le fit valdinguer et glisser sur le sol.
– Aouh !… gémit le crocodile.
Au secours ! arrêtez !
où suis-je ?

– Eh regarde ! cria Julien. Cet arbre, là-bas,
est beaucoup plus petit que les autres
et il est couvert de noix de coco ! Je dois pouvoir
y grimper si tu me donnes un coup de main.

Julien et Marie se précipitent vers ce qu'ils
pensent être un petit cocotier. L'Énorme
Crocodile épie à travers les branches, suivant
des yeux les enfants à mesure qu'ils approchent.
Il se lèche les babines. Le voilà qui bave
d'excitation…

Il rassembla les branches et les serra entre
ses dents. Il recueillit les noix de coco dans
ses pattes de devant. Puis il se dressa en prenant
équilibre sur sa queue. Il avait disposé
les branches et les noix de coco si habilement
qu'il ressemblait à présent à un petit cocotier
perdu parmi de grands cocotiers.
Bientôt arrivèrent deux enfants : le frère
et la sœur. Le garçon s'appelait Julien ;
la fillette, Marie. Ils inspectèrent les lieux,
à la recherche de noix de coco, mais ils
n'en purent trouver aucune, car l'Énorme
Crocodile les avait toutes ramassées.

Cette marche à travers la jungle m'a donné
une faim de loup. Un enfant, ça ne me suffira
pas aujourd'hui. Je ne serai rassasié qu'après
en avoir dévoré au moins trois, bien juteux ! »
Il se mit à ramper en direction de la ville.

L'Énorme Crocodile parvint à un endroit
où il y avait de nombreux cocotiers. Il savait
que les enfants y venaient souvent chercher
des noix de coco. Les arbres étaient trop grands
pour qu'ils puissent y grimper, mais il y avait
toujours des noix de coco à terre.
L'Énorme Crocodile ramassa à la hâte toutes
celles qui jonchaient le sol, ainsi que plusieurs
branches cassées.
« Et maintenant, passons au piège subtil n° 1,
murmura-t-il, je n'aurai pas à attendre longtemps
avant de goûter au premier plat. »

Finalement, l'Énorme Crocodile parvint
de l'autre côté de la jungle, dans un rayon
de soleil.
Il pouvait apercevoir la ville, toute proche.
« Ho, ho ! se confia-t-il à haute voix, ha, ha !

Dodu-de-la-Plume poussa un cri d'horreur
et fendit l'air comme une flèche, abandonnant
les plumes de sa queue dans la gueule
de l'Énorme Crocodile.

L'Énorme Crocodile éclata d'un si grand rire
que ses dents cliquetèrent telles des pièces
dans une tirelire.
— Les crocodiles ne mangent pas de baies,
affirma-t-il. Nous mangeons les petits garçons
et les petites filles. Parfois, aussi, les oiseaux.
D'une brusque détente, il se dressa et lança
ses mâchoires vers Dodu-de-la-Plume.
Il le manqua de peu mais parvint à saisir
les longues et magnifiques plumes de sa queue.

L'arbre s'écrasa au sol, mais Jojo-la-Malice
bondit à temps vers les branches voisines
et s'enfuit dans le feuillage.

Un peu plus loin, l'Énorme Crocodile rencontra
Dodu-de-la-Plume, l'oiseau.
Dodu-de-la-Plume bâtissait un nid dans un
oranger.
– Salut à toi, Énorme Crocodile ! chanta Dodu-
de-la-Plume. On ne te voit pas souvent par ici.
– Ah, dit le Crocodile. J'ai dressé des plans
secrets et mis au point des ruses habiles.
– Rien de mauvais ? chanta Dodu-de-la-Plume.
– Mauvais ! ricana le Crocodile. Sûrement pas
mauvais ! au contraire, c'est délicieux !

C'est succulent, c'est super,
C'est fondant, c'est hyper !
Et c'est bien meilleur qu'du vieux poisson pourri
Ça s'écrase et ça craque,
Ça s'mastique et ça se croque !
D'l'entendre crisser sous la dent c'est joli !

– Ce doit être des baies, siffla Dodu-de-la-Plume.
Pour moi, les baies, c'est ce qu'il y a de meilleur
au monde.
Peut-être des framboises ? Ou des fraises ?

– Veux-tu des noisettes ? demanda Jojo-la-Malice.
– J'ai mieux que ça, dit le Crocodile avec
dédain.
– Y a-t-il quelque chose de meilleur que
les noisettes ? interrogea Jojo-la-Malice.
– Ha, ha ! fit l'Énorme Crocodile.

**L'aliment que je m'en vais consommer
Possède doigts, ongles, bras, jambes, pieds !**

Jojo-la-Malice pâlit et frémit de la tête
aux pieds.
– Tu n'as pas réellement l'intention d'engloutir
un enfant, non ? s'effraya-t-il.
– Bien sûr que si, assura le Crocodile.
Les vêtements et tout. C'est meilleur avec
les vêtements.
– Oh, l'horrible goinfre, s'indigna
Jojo-la-Malice. Le répugnant personnage !
je voudrais que boutons et boucles te restent
en travers de la gorge et t'étouffent !

Le Crocodile s'esclaffa :
– Je mange également les singes.
Et, rapide comme l'éclair, d'un coup sec
de ses terribles mâchoires, il brisa l'arbre
sur lequel se tenait Jojo-la-Malice.

Un peu plus loin, il rencontra Jojo-la-Malice,
le singe. Jojo-la-Malice, perché sur un arbre,
mangeait des noisettes.

– Salut, Croquette, dit Jojo-la-Malice.
Qu'est-ce que tu fabriques ?

– J'ai dressé des plans secrets et mis au point
des ruses habiles.

– Ah, quelle brute épaisse ! s'emporta
Trompette. Ah, quel infect, ignoble monstre !
Je voudrais que tu sois brisé et broyé, bouilli
et réduit en ragoût de crocodile !

L'Énorme Crocodile partit d'un rire bruyant
et moqueur et s'enfonça dans l'épaisse jungle.

– Tu ne veux pas dire…, s'inquiéta Double-Croupe. Tu ne vas pas me dire que tu veux manger un enfant !

– Mais si ! acquiesça le Crocodile.

– Ah le sale vorace ! la sombre brute ! s'emporta Double-Croupe. J'espère que tu seras capturé, qu'on te fera cuire et que tu seras transformé en soupe de crocodile !!!

L'Énorme Crocodile partit d'un rire bruyant et moqueur, puis il s'enfonça dans la jungle.

Dans la jungle, il rencontra Trompette, l'éléphant. Trompette grignotait des feuilles cueillies à la cime d'un grand arbre et il ne remarqua pas tout d'abord le Crocodile.

Aussi ce dernier le mordit-il à la jambe.

– Eh, s'offusqua Trompette de sa grosse voix profonde. Qui se permet ? Ah, c'est toi, affreux Crocodile. Pourquoi ne retournes-tu pas à cette grande rivière noire et boueuse d'où tu viens ?

– J'ai dressé des plans secrets et mis au point des ruses habiles, dit le Crocodile.

– Tu veux dire de sombres plans et des ruses sournoises, insinua Trompette. De ta vie, tu n'as accompli une seule bonne action.

L'Énorme Crocodile s'esclaffa :

J'suis d'sortie pour trouver un gosse à croquer.
Tends l'oreille et t'entendras les os craquer !

C'était Double-Croupe, l'hippopotame.

– Salut, salut ! dit Double-Croupe. Où vas-tu
à cette heure du jour ?

– J'ai dressé des plans secrets et mis au point
des ruses habiles.

– Hélas ! s'exclama Double-Croupe, je jurerais
que tu as en tête quelque horrible projet.

L'Énorme Crocodile rit à belles dents :

J'vais remplir mon ventre affamé et creux
Avec un truc délicieux, délicieux.

– Qu'est-ce qui est si délicieux ? interrogea
Double-Croupe.

– Devine, lança le crocodile. C'est quelque
chose qui marche sur deux jambes.

L'Énorme Crocodile s'esclaffa de nouveau,
et ses terribles dents blanches et pointues
étincelèrent comme des couteaux au soleil.
– Personne ne me verra, dit-il, parce que cette
fois, j'ai dressé des plans secrets et mis au point
des ruses habiles.
– Des ruses habiles ? s'écria le Pas-si-Gros.
Tu n'as jamais rien fait d'habile de toute ta vie !
Tu es le plus stupide croco de toute la rivière !
– Je suis le croco le plus malin de toute
la rivière, répondit l'Énorme Crocodile.
Ce midi, je me régalerai d'un petit enfant dodu
et bien juteux pendant que toi,
tu resteras ici, le ventre vide. Au revoir.

L'Énorme Crocodile gagna la rive et se hissa
hors de l'eau. Une gigantesque créature
pataugeait dans la boue visqueuse de la berge.

– Les enfants sont plus gros que les poissons,
rétorqua l'Énorme Crocodile. Ça te fait
de plus grosses parts.
– Tu es un sale glouton, lança le Pas-si-Gros.
Tu es le croco le plus glouton de toute
la rivière.
– Je suis le croco le plus audacieux de toute
la rivière, affirma l'Énorme Crocodile.
Je suis le seul à oser quitter la rivière,
à traverser la jungle jusqu'à la ville pour
y chercher des petits enfants à manger.
– Ça ne t'est arrivé qu'une seule fois, grogna
le Pas-si-Gros. Et que se passa-t-il alors ?
Tous les enfants t'ont vu venir et se sont enfuis.
– Oh mais, aujourd'hui, il n'est pas question
qu'ils me voient, répliqua l'Énorme Crocodile.
– Bien sûr qu'ils te verront, reprit le Pas-si-Gros,
tu es si énorme et si laid qu'ils t'apercevront
à des kilomètres.

– Coriaces ! élastiques !! s'offusqua l'Énorme Crocodile. Écœurants ! amers !!! tu racontes des bêtises grosses comme toi. Ils sont juteux et délicieux !

– Ils ont un goût si amer, insista le Pas-si-Gros, qu'il faut les enduire de sucre avant de les consommer.

L'Énorme Crocodile s'esclaffa, découvrant
des centaines de dents blanches et pointues.
– Pour mon déjeuner aujourd'hui, reprit-il,
j'aimerais un joli petit garçon bien juteux.
– Je ne mange jamais d'enfants,
dit le Pas-si-Gros. Seulement du poisson.
– Ho, ho, ho ! s'écria l'Énorme Crocodile.
Je suis prêt à parier que si tu voyais, à ce moment
précis, un petit garçon dodu et bien juteux
barboter dans l'eau, tu n'en ferais qu'une
bouchée !
– Certes pas ! répondit le Pas-si-Gros.
Les enfants sont trop coriaces et trop élastiques.
Ils sont coriaces, élastiques, écœurants et amers.

Au milieu de la plus grande, la plus noire,
la plus boueuse rivière d'Afrique, deux crocodiles
se prélassaient, la tête à fleur d'eau. L'un des
crocodiles était énorme. L'autre n'était pas si gros.
– Sais-tu ce que j'aimerais pour mon déjeuner
aujourd'hui ? demanda l'Énorme Crocodile.
– Non, dit le Pas-si-Gros. Quoi ?

Roald Dahl · Quentin Blake

L'Énorme Crocodile

GALLIMARD JEUNESSE